GU00984832

365 DAYS OF
SALAD
RECIPES

Emma Katie

Copyright © 2016 Emma Katie

All rights reserved.

This book is licensed for your personal enjoyment only. This book may not be re-sold or given away to other people. If you would like to share this book with another person, please purchase an additional copy for each recipient. If you're reading this book and did not purchase it, or it was not purchased for your enjoyment only, then please return to your favorite retailer and purchase your own copy. Thank you for respecting the hard work of this author.

No part of this book may be reproduced in any form or by any electronic or mechanical means, including information storage and retrieval systems, without written permission from the author, except for the use of brief quotations in a book review. If you would like to use material from the book (other than just simply for reviewing the book), prior permission must be obtained by contacting the author at emma.katie@outlook.com.

Check out more books by Emma Katie at:
www.amazon.com/author/emmakatie

ISBN-13: 978-1539581468

Contents

Introduction

There are numerous salad recipes, which are not only mouthwatering, but delicious and also help you stay healthy and have a controlled balanced diet. Every human being needs vitamins proteins and nutrients to maintain a good health. Thus, I have made a perfect book of 365 days of Salad Recipes, which contains highly nutritious salad recipes which make your food taste better and are easy to serve. Your family and kids would love to have these every day. These dishes can be made from vegetables, which are easily available at any kind of market. The preparation is also very simple and unique, so that you can not only prepare the salad perfectly but also make the salad taste better. Every recipe is tested and can be cooked at home without any high technical methods. The recipes are written in an easy way so that you can understand the exact way to prepare the delicious dishes. The book is written with the exact picture of the dishes. The ingredients are also given with exact measurements to give you the perfect amount of dish to prepare. The book also includes tips and other exciting features like step-by-step recipes, which make the users to prepare the dishes perfectly. A few tips are also shared with you here to help you in your endeavor. You will find unique salad recipes like the following:

Apricot and blue berry Salsa

Spicy carrot salad

Squash and orzo salad

Pasta and Black Eyed Peas in Salad

And many others

Sample Tips:

Garnish the salad with hazel nuts or melon nuts to make the taste crunchy and nutty

You can also add whipped cream or sour cream to make the texture creamier

You can add sugar free cubes too in place of sour or whipped cream

The salt, pepper, lime, cheese, oils and other dressing ingredients can be used as per taste, hence no quantity mentioned

365 days of Salad recipes

Spanish Salad

Ingredients

2 Chopped scallions
2 Pimientos
1 Fresh romaine
6 Olives
1 tsp. Paprika
2 Cloves of garlic
Drizzle of Balsamic vinegar
4 Blanched almonds
2 Bread slices
Pinch of salt to taste

Method

Firstly, preheat the oven. Then grease the grill a bit. Chop the scallions very finely. Now put them in the preheated oven. After they are ready, take them in a mixing bowl and add the fresh romaine, pimientos, olives, and almonds to the bowl. Toss well. Now, add the Balsamic vinegar and sprinkle paprika and salt to taste. Rub the grilled bread slices with garlic and crumble them in the bowl. Toss well. Enjoy!

Avocado salad

Ingredients

2 fresh avocados
1 freshly chopped sweet onion
1 Finely chopped bell pepper, green
Fresh cilantro, chopped

Juice of 1/2 lemon
Salt to taste
Freshly ground black pepper to sprinkle

Method

Take all the fresh ingredients. Wash them. Now take a mixing salad bowl. Now add the peeled, pitted and well diced avocado, chopped sweet onion, chopped green bell pepper, and freshly chopped cilantro. Then drizzle fresh lime juice of about half a lemon. Then for seasoning sprinkle salt to taste and freshly ground black pepper. Then toss them very well and serve them fresh and delicious. Enjoy!

Waldorf salad

Ingredients

1/2 cup of mayonnaise
¼ cup Fresh sour cream
¼ cup Chives
1 bunch Fresh parsley, chopped
1 tsp. Lemon zest

Fresh juice of 1/2 a lime
1 tsp. Celery
8 Walnuts
Sugar to taste
Freshly ground black pepper to sprinkle

Method

Take a bowl and pour the mayonnaise and whisk it with fresh sour cream. Now add the chives, freshly chopped parsley and lemon zest. Mix them well. Drizzle the fresh lime juice and sprinkle sugar according to your desire and pepper for seasoning. Toss with chopped celery and walnuts. Enjoy!

Fruit Salad

Ingredients

2 Fresh red apples
1 cup Cranberries
2-3 stalks of celery

½ cup Chopped walnuts
1 nectarine
Fresh yogurt, according to taste

Method

Take the fresh red apples and chop them well. Chop the walnuts and celery as well. Now take a large mixing salad bowl. Now add the pieces of red apple, Cranberries, Dried or fresh , nectarine, chopped walnuts and chopped fresh celery. Toss well. Now pour the fresh yogurt into the bowl and mix well. Refrigerate the salad for about 3 hours. Serve chilled. Enjoy!

Greek salad with Rice

Ingredients

½ cup extra virgin olive oil
2 cup cooked rice
1 Fresh cucumber
2 fresh tomatoes
1 bunch fresh parsley
1 bunch mint

1 tsp. dried dill
½ cup Feta cheese
½ cup chopped scallions
Hot sauce, to taste
Salt, to taste
2 tbsp. lemon juice

Lemon zest, to taste

Method

Take a bowl, and whisk extra virgin olive oil, fresh lemon juice and salt to taste. Chop fresh cucumbers and tomatoes. Add them to the olive oil and lemon juice mix and toss to coat. Now add chopped parsley, dried dill, scallions, fresh mint and lemon zest of half a lemon and mix well. Now add in the cooked rice and mix gently to make sure the rice doesn't break up. Top it up with hot sauce and feta cheese. Serve immediately. Enjoy!

Mango Salsa Salad

Ingredients

1 chopped mango
1 Chopped green onion
3 tbsp. freshly chopped cilantro

3 tbsp. of lemon juice
1 Chopped red bell paper
1 Fine chopped fresh jalapeno pepper

Method

Wash the mango, peel and chop it .Take a mixing bowl and add the mangos, red bell pepper, chopped green onion, freshly chopped cilantro and finely chopped jalapeno pepper. Mix them well. Cover the bowl and allow the mixture to soak in the juices for 30-40 minutes. Place this salsa out in a serving dish and serve it with chips or with fish. Enjoy!

Red Bean Salad

Ingredients

15 ounces of kidney beans
1 Chopped bell pepper
1 cup Feta cheese
Drizzle of olive oil
1 Minced clove of garlic

1 head Chopped cabbage
1 tsp. Fresh parsley, Chopped
Drizzle of olive oil
Drizzle of fresh lemon juice

Method

First, take the canned kidney beans and rinse well for a few minutes. In a large salad mixing bowl, add the kidney beans, chopped cabbage, onions, bell pepper and minced clove of garlic. Toss together. Then add the parsley, lemon juice and drizzle olive oil and mix until coated. Top it with feta cheese. Refrigerate for few hours and serve chilled. Enjoy!

Dill and Butter Squash Salad

Ingredients

1 fresh sliced zucchini
2 fresh yellow squash
2-3 tsp. of dried dill weed
1 tbsp. Lemon juice

Salt to taste
Pepper
2 tsp. Butter

Method

Wash and chop the zucchini and squash. Heat butter in a pan and sauté the vegetables on low-medium heat for 10-15 minutes. Season the vegetables with a pinch of salt and pepper and dried dill weed. Then sauté for some more time and add the lemon juice. Refrigerate overnight and serve chilled. Enjoy!

Fresh cucumber yogurt salad

Ingredients

1 cup Plain yogurt
3-4 English cucumbers
Salt
Pepper

1 tsp. Dried dill weed
1 finely chopped shallot
1 clove of garlic minced

Method

Wash the English cucumbers, peel and chop them. Chop the shallot finely. Now take a mixing bowl and add the chopped cucumbers, shallot, yogurt and garlic and mix them thoroughly. Sprinkle salt, pepper and dried dill weed. Toss the salad well. Refrigerate overnight and serve chilled. Enjoy!

Easy Macaroni Salad

Ingredients

1 cup cooked macaroni
½ cup mayonnaise
3 tbsp. fresh sour cream
1 tsp. dried mustard
1 stalk celery, sliced
1 red onion, chopped
1 tsp. chopped parsley

Sugar, to taste
Drizzle of cider vinegar
Salt to taste
Freshly ground black pepper for seasoning

Method

Take a bowl and whisk mayonnaise along with the fresh sour cream. Add the dried mustard, drizzle of cider vinegar, sugar, salt and freshly ground black pepper to taste. Mix well. Toss in the cooked macaroni and freshly sliced onion, parsley and celery and mix well. Serve immediately. Enjoy!

Greek Salad with Omelet

Ingredients

5 eggs
1 tbsp. olive oil
½ red onion
2 tomatoes, cut into chunks

5-6 Black olives
1 tsp. chopped parsley
½ cup crumbled feta cheese
Salt and pepper

Method

Take a large bowl and whisk the eggs in it with salt, pepper and chopped parsley. Heat the olive oil in a non-stick pan and fry the red onions for few minutes, until tender. Add tomatoes and olives to the pan and cook for a few minutes. Now, pour the whisked egg into it and cook until done. Scatter the feta cheese on the top and place the pan on the pre-heated grill for 6 minutes. Now, cut the puffed and golden omelet into wedges and serve it. Enjoy!

Bacon and Pea Salad

Ingredients

4 Slices of bacon
1/4 cup water
2 Fresh onions, finely chopped

1 pack of frozen green peas
A drizzle of Ranch dressing
1/2 cup of cheddar cheese, shredded

Method

Brown the bacon in a pan and crumble when cooked. Keep aside. Boil the pack of green peas in a pot and drain. Cool them. Now take a mixing bowl and combine the crumbled bacon, green peas, onion, ranch dressing and shredded cheddar. Toss them all well and then put in refrigerator for an hour. Serve chilled. Enjoy!

Simple Yellow Salad

Ingredients

1 cob of Yellow corn
Drizzle of extra virgin olive oil
1 Fresh yellow squash
3 Fresh yellow grape tomatoes

3-4 Fresh basil leaves
Pinch of salt to taste
Freshly ground black pepper to sprinkle

Method

Firstly, cut the kernels off the corn. Cut the fresh yellow squash and fresh yellow grape tomatoes into slices. Now take a skillet and drizzle some olive oil and sauté the corn and squash until tender. In a bowl, add all the ingredients and season to taste. Toss and serve. Enjoy!

Citrus and Basil Salad

Ingredients

Extra virgin olive oil
2 Oranges, juiced
1 Fresh lemon juice
1 Lemon zest

1 tbsp. of honey
Drizzle of white wine vinegar
Pinch of salt
2-3 Fresh basil leaves, chopped

Method

Take a large salad mixing bowl and add the extra virgin olive oil, fresh lemon and orange juice and mix well. Then add lemon zest, honey, white wine vinegar, fresh basil leaves and sprinkle some salt over them to taste. Toss well to mix. Then put in the refrigerator to chill and serve. Enjoy!

Simple Pretzel Salad

Ingredients

1 Pack of pretzels
Salt to sprinkle
2/3 cup Peanut oil

Garlic and herb salad dressing, you can use salad dressing of your own choice , according to taste

Method

Take a large mixing bag. Now add the pretzels, peanut oil, the garlic and herb salad dressing mixture or any other salad dressing. Sprinkle some salt to season. Now shake the bag well so that the pretzels are uniformly coated. Serve it immediately. Enjoy!

Butternut Squash Salad

Ingredients

2 boxes of Butternut squash, Cubed
Drizzle of Extra virgin olive oil

Pinch of salt to taste
Freshly ground black pepper for seasoning

Method

Take about 2 boxes of butternut squash, wash and cube them well. Now, preheat the oven to about 400 degrees F. Take the butternut squash in a bowl, drizzle some extra virgin olive oil and sprinkle a pinch of salt and freshly ground black pepper on them. Toss them well so that all the cubes get uniformly coated. Roast butternut till they soften and top caramelizes. Serve. Enjoy!

Tomato, Radish and Cucumber Salad

Ingredients

2-3 large tomatoes
1-2 cucumbers
2 radishes, thinly sliced
2 red and orange bell peppers
Pepper to taste

1 bunch green onions, finely chopped
Drizzle of canola oil
Drizzle of White vinegar
Salt to sprinkle

Method

Wash all the vegetables, chop them finely and place in a bowl. Drizzle some canola oil and white vinegar. Toss them well so that all the vegetables get evenly coated. Now sprinkle some salt and freshly ground black pepper and toss again. Serve this fresh salad immediately with bread or chips or with any meal. Enjoy!

Fresh Tomato and Avocado Salad with Dijon Mustard

Ingredients

2 fresh tomatoes
1 Avocado
1 tsp. of Dijon Mustard
Balsamic vinegar, to taste

Freshly ground black pepper
Little drizzle of extra virgin olive oil

Method

Cut the tomatoes into wedges and peel the avocado, pit and slice it. Take a bowl and mix together the Dijon mustard, a drizzle olive oil, balsamic vinegar to taste and some black pepper. Take a big serving plate and arrange the slices of tomatoes and avocados in it. Now drizzle the dressing that you have prepared over them. Serve this salad immediately. Enjoy!

Simple Jicama Salad

Ingredients

1 jicama, also known as yam bean
Salt to taste

Drizzle of fresh lime juice
Sprinkle of Chili powder

Method

Peel a jicama and cut into small pieces. Arrange the jicama in a large serving plate. Sprinkle fresh lime juice, salt and chili powder on the pieces of jicama. Serve immediately. Enjoy!

Fresh Radish and Dill Salad

Ingredients

1 fresh Radish
1½ tsp. of finely chopped dill
3 tsp. white vinegar
Canola oil to drizzle

Pinch of salt
Black pepper, ground
Method

Peel and slice the radish finely. Take the slices in a bowl and add a pinch of salt. Toss well. Let it sit for about 10-12 minutes. Then pour some white vinegar, add the chopped dill, drizzle canola oil and sprinkle pepper. Mix well and serve the dish immediately. Enjoy!

Green Bean and Cabbage Salad

Ingredients

12 ounces of fresh green beans
1 cup Feta cheese, You can also use Mozzarella
Drizzle of olive oil
1 clove of garlic minced

1 fresh Cabbage
1 tsp. Fresh parsley, Chopped
Drizzle of olive oil
Drizzle of fresh lemon juice

Method

Wash and drain the green beans. In a large salad mixing bowl, add the green beans, chopped cabbage, onions, garlic, parsley, lemon juice and drizzle olive oil. Toss well. Top it with feta cheese. Refrigerate to cool and serve. Enjoy!

Lemony Tangy Cucumber Salad

Ingredients

2-3 fresh cucumbers, finely sliced
2 tsp. white wine vinegar
3 tsp. celery seeds
Salt t, to taste

Fresh black pepper, to taste
4 tbsp. fresh lemon juice
1 chopped onion

Method

Place the cucumbers in salad mixing bowl. Add the white vinegar, celery seeds, onion, lemon juice and sprinkle some salt and some black pepper. Combine everything thoroughly and then put into the freezer. Serve chilled. Enjoy!

Green Pea Salad with Egg

Ingredients

2 cans fresh green peas
3-4 eggs
4 tbsp. fresh lemon juice
1 tsp. fresh cilantro, chopped

2 fresh onions, chopped
6 cherry tomatoes, cut in halves
Salt to taste
Garlic powder to taste

Method

Mix together the peas, onions, cherry tomatoes, and fresh cilantro. Now squeeze in fresh lemon juice, add some salt, and garlic powder. Mix well. Boil the eggs to make some hard boiled eggs and cut them into halves and add to the salad bowl. Serve immediately. Enjoy!

Cherry Tomato and Bacon salad

Ingredients

2 fresh cherry tomatoes, cut them into halves
5 slices of bacons

Freshly ground black pepper to taste
Garlic salt to taste
½ cup crumbled fresh mozzarella or feta

cheese   Some fresh basil leaves

Method

Cook the slices of bacon until brown, crumble them and keep them in a bowl. Now in a salad mixing bowl, add the halved cherry tomatoes and fresh basil leaves along with crumbled fresh mozzarella or feta cheese over them. Spread the crumbled bacon. Top up with pepper and garlic salt. Serve immediately. Enjoy!

Fresh and Easy Chickpea Salad

Ingredients

1 can chickpeas   2 cucumbers, chopped
2 red onions, chopped   1 tsp. chili powder
2 tomatoes, chopped   Some salt

Method

Boil the chickpeas in a pot until tender. Place in a mixing bowl with the tomatoes, red onions and cucumber pieces. Combine all of them together very well. Season with salt and chili powder and mix well. Serve it immediately. Enjoy!

Hardboiled Egg Salad

Ingredients

4-5 hardboiled eggs, chopped   Pinch of garlic salt to taste
1 Avocado   Freshly ground black pepper to sprinkle
Dijon mustard, to taste

Method

Take a bowl and add the pieces of eggs, Dijon mustard, avocado and mash them well together. Sprinkle some garlic salt and pepper to season. Mix them well and serve immediately. Enjoy!

Tasty Pasta Salad

Ingredients

Cooked Pasta½ cup of mayonnaise   1 celery stalk, sliced
3 tbsp. Fresh sour cream   1 red onion, chopped
1 tsp. Dried mustard   1 tsp. parsley, chopped

Sugar to taste
2 tbsp. White or cider vinegar

Salt, to taste
Freshly ground black pepper, to taste

Method

Take a bowl and whisk mayonnaise along with about fresh sour cream. Add in the dried mustard, drizzle of cider or white vinegar, sugar and sprinkle salt and fresh ground black pepper to taste and mix well. Add the cooked pasta and sliced onion, parsley and celery. Toss them well and serve. Enjoy!

Mushroom and Baby Corn Salad with couscous

Ingredients

1 cup Couscous
5-6 Mushrooms
1 peeled tomato

7-8 Baby corn
Salt
Black or white pepper

Method

Take a pot with water and add the couscous and bring to boil. When the couscous is cooked drain it well. Meanwhile chop the mushrooms and take in a bowl. Add tomatoes, and baby corn to the mushrooms and microwave for 2 to 3 minutes. Now mix these with the cooked couscous. Mix them well and sprinkle salt and black or white pepper. Serve immediately. Enjoy!

Carrot Salad with Ginger and Lemon

Ingredients

2 carrots
2 cloves of garlic, minced
1 tsp. cinnamon powder
1/2 inch piece of ginger, grated finely

Salt, to taste
Black pepper, to taste
Drizzle of oil

Method

Wash, peel and slice the carrots and place on a plate. In a bowl, add the grated ginger, garlic, drizzle of oil, cinnamon powder and some pepper and salt. Mix them well. Now spread this mixture with the carrots. Serve immediately. Enjoy!

Jicama and Water Melon Salad

Ingredients

1 Jicama
1 Watermelon
3 tbsp. fresh lime juice
Lemon zest

2 tsp. Honey
1 tbsp. fresh mint leaves, chopped
Salt and pepper to taste

Method

Cut the jicama into slices and the watermelon into cubes. Place the jicama and water melon in a bowl. Add in the lemon juice, lemon zest, honey and mint. Toss them together so that jicama and watermelons get coated uniformly. Taste and season accordingly. Now refrigerate the salad for about 2 hours and then serve to all. Enjoy!

Fresh Beet Salad

Ingredients

1 fresh beets, roasted
1tsp. dried mustard powder
Salt
2 onions, chopped

1½ tbsp. poppy seeds
Sugar, to taste
1½ tsp. vegetable oil
½ cup crumbled Feta cheese

Method

Combine all the ingredients in a bowl and toss well till all the ingredients are mixed properly. Serve immediately. Enjoy!

Summer Fresh Cucumber and Watermelon Salad

Ingredients

2 fresh cucumbers, sliced
1 fresh watermelon, cubed
Pinch of salt to taste

Drizzle of Balsamic vinegar
1 tsp. Sugar

Method

Combine all the ingredients in a bowl and toss well till all the ingredients are mixed properly. Refrigerate and serve. Enjoy!

Tasty Onion and Celery Salad

Ingredients

1 stalk celery, chopped
2 onions, diced
2 tbsp. Lemon juice
Drizzle of olive oil

5-6 basil leaves
Pinch of salt
Ground pepper, to taste

Method

Combine all the ingredients in a bowl and toss well till all the ingredients are mixed properly. Refrigerate and serve. Enjoy!

Spinach and Red Onion Salad

Ingredients

1 bunch fresh baby spinach
2 red onions, finely chopped
3 cucumbers, chopped
Crumble some slice of bacons, if you

desire
½ cup Fresh Mozzarella cheese
Oregano, to taste

Method

Combine all the ingredients, except for the cheese, in a bowl and toss well till all the ingredients are mixed properly. Refrigerate and serve topped with the cheese. Enjoy!

Watermelon Topped with Mozzarella

Ingredients

1 Fresh watermelon
5 to 6 fresh Basil leaves
1 tbsp. balsamic vinegar

1 cup Mozzarella cheese
Oregano for seasoning

Method

Combine all the ingredients in a bowl and toss well till all the ingredients are mixed properly. Taste and season accordingly. Refrigerate and serve. Enjoy!

Tasty Low-Carb Bacon Salad

Ingredients

½ cup of mayonnaise
1 crushed clove of garlic
½ cup lettuce
Salt

Fresh ground black pepper, to taste
4 tbsp. lime juice
1 tbsp. anchovy paste
5 slices of bacon

Method

First take a frying pan and fry the slices of bacon until they become crispy. Cool them and crumble them. Now in a bowl add mayonnaise, garlic salt and pepper and anchovy paste to it. Mix well to form a dressing. Add the fresh lettuce and toss well to coat. Season to taste. Serve topped with the crumbled bacon. Enjoy!

Fresh Carrot and Cucumber Salad

Ingredients

2 carrots, sliced and roasted
2 cucumbers, sliced
2 tsp. dried mustard powder
Salt
1½ tbsp. poppy seeds

Sugar, to taste
1 1/2 tsp. vegetable oil
½ cup crumbled Feta cheese or mozzarella cheese

Method

Combine all the ingredients in a bowl and toss well till all the ingredients are mixed properly. Serve immediately. Enjoy!

Morning fresh Jicama and Mango salad

Ingredients

2 fresh mangoes, cubed
1 fresh Jicama, cubed
6-8 fresh mint leaves

Pinch of salt to taste
Drizzle of Balsamic vinegar

Method

Combine all the ingredients in a bowl and toss well till all the ingredients are mixed properly. Refrigerate and serve. Enjoy!

Healthy and Fresh Tuna Salad

Ingredients

1 mashed avocado
1 scallion, sliced
1 can of tuna
Lime juice, as required

2 tomatoes, finely chopped
Capers, as per taste
Salt to taste
Pepper to taste

Method

Mash the avocado with a fork. Add lime juice to it till the consistency is smooth. Now fold in the chopped tomatoes, drained tuna, capers and scallion into the mashed avocado. Season with salt and black pepper to taste. Serve this delicious tuna salad with chips or with vegetables or on a bed of greens. Enjoy!

Simple Green Beans, Celery and Olive Salad

Ingredients

1 packet Fresh green beans
1 stalk celery, diced
Lemon juice, as required
Drizzle of olive oil

2 basil leaves
5 Olives
Pinch of salt, to taste
Pepper, to taste

Method

Combine all the ingredients in a bowl and toss well till all the ingredients are mixed properly. Refrigerate and serve. Enjoy!

Spinach Salad with Fresh Mint and Avocado

Ingredients

1 bunch Fresh baby spinach
Fresh mint, as per taste
2 avocados, sliced
2 red onions, finely chopped

2 cucumbers, chopped
1 cup Mozzarella cheese
Oregano for taste

Method

Combine all the ingredients in a bowl and toss well till all the ingredients are mixed properly. Refrigerate and serve. Enjoy!

Fresh Sugar Snaps with Mozzarella

Ingredients

1 cup fresh sugar snaps
4 dried cranberries
1 sprig basil leaves
1 sprig mint leaves

Balsamic vinegar, to taste
½ cup fresh Mozzarella cheese
Oregano for seasoning

Method

Combine all the ingredients in a bowl and toss well till all the ingredients are mixed properly. Refrigerate and serve. Enjoy!

Tuna Salad with Eggs and Apples

Ingredients

1 tuna packed in olive oil
1 fresh green onion, chopped finely
1 apple, sliced
3-4 Hard-boiled eggs

1 tbsp. celery
2 tbsp. cream dressing
Freshly ground black pepper, to taste
Salt, to taste

Method

Combine all the ingredients in a bowl and toss well till all the ingredients are mixed properly. Refrigerate and serve. Enjoy!

Beet and Walnut with Prunes

Ingredients

2 beets, grated
8 prunes, chopped
2 cloves of garlic, minced
Salt, to taste

1½ tbsp. chopped walnuts
Sugar, as per taste
½ tsp. vegetable oil
½ cup Feta cheese or mozzarella

Method

Combine all the ingredients in a bowl and toss well till all the ingredients are mixed properly. Serve immediately. Enjoy!

Broccoli florets with Onions and pine nuts

Ingredients

2 cups broccoli florets
1 handful pine nuts
2 red onions, chopped
6-8 mint leaves

2 tsp. balsamic vinegar
½ cup Fresh Mozzarella cheese
Oregano for seasoning

Method

Combine all the ingredients in a bowl and toss well till all the ingredients are mixed properly. Refrigerate and serve chilled. Enjoy!

Tofu salad over baby spinach

Ingredients

1 Tofu, cubed
1 bunch baby spinach
2-3 pieces of ginger
1/4 cup water

1/2 tsp. Rice wine vinegar
Red chili paste, as per taste
Oil to drizzle
1/2 tsp. soy sauce

Method

Puree the ginger with the water, rice wine vinegar, soy sauce and vegetable oil. Combine the tofu and spinach in a bowl and spoon in the ginger mix onto them. Enjoy!

Asparagus salad with tasty bacons

Ingredients

1 bunch asparagus, trimmed
1 cup Bacon, crumbled
Drizzle of olive oil
Balsamic vinegar to taste

1 tsp. Soy sauce
Pinch of salt
Ground black pepper

Method

Firstly trim the fresh asparagus and boil them till they are crisp and tender and keep them aside. Now in a small mixing bowl, add some oil, some soy sauce and balsamic vinegar and sprinkle some amount of salt and black ground pepper to taste. Mix them very well. Now in a salad bowl add the asparagus and this dressing and mix. Then add crumbled cooked bacon pieces and serve immediately. Enjoy!

Easy crabmeat salad

Ingredients

1 lump of crab meat
1 stalk celery
½ cup mayonnaise
1 tsp. tarragon

2 chives, chopped
1/4 cup fresh sour cream
1 tsp. dried mustard
Fresh lime juice of 1/2 a lemon

Method

First take a deep bowl and mix the lump of crab meat along with the celery and chives and tarragon. Mix them well. Add the mayonnaise, fresh sour cream, and dried mustard and drizzle the lime juice. Now mix them all very thoroughly. Serve immediately. Enjoy!

Strawberry and onions tossed in red wine

Ingredients

4-5 strawberries, sliced
2 red onions, sliced
½ cup Mayonnaise
¼ of a cup of fresh sour cream

Drizzle of red wine
Some poppy seeds, as per taste
½ cup of white sugar

Method

Combine all the ingredients in a bowl and toss well till all the ingredients are mixed properly. Refrigerate and serve chilled. Enjoy!

Bulgur with pea nuts and scallions

Ingredients

2 cups cooked bulgur
½ cup peanuts, toasted
2 sprigs scallions
Extra virgin olive oil
2 tomatoes, diced
Fresh parsley
Fresh mint leaves

Salt, to taste
Black pepper, to taste

Method

Combine all the ingredients in a bowl and toss well till all the ingredients are mixed properly. Refrigerate and serve chilled. Enjoy!

Cornbread crumbs with Tofu salad

Ingredients

1 cup cornbread crumbs
1 Tofu, cubed
2-3 pieces of ginger
Water- as required

2 tsp. white wine vinegar
1 tsp. red chili paste
Oil to drizzle
1 tsp. soy sauce

Method

Take the gingers in a blender and convert into puree by adding some water, white wine vinegar, soy sauce and oil to it. Now once this puree is prepared and spread it over the cornbread crumbs and tofu. Enjoy!

Tasty bacons with greens

Ingredients

1 bunch trimmed asparagus
1 bunch Baby spinach
1 slice Bacon, crumbled
Drizzle of olive oil

Balsamic vinegar to taste
1 tsp. Soy sauce
Pinch of salt
Ground black pepper

Method

Boil the asparagus till they become tender. In a small mixing bowl, add some oil, some soy sauce and balsamic vinegar and sprinkle some amount of salt and black ground pepper to taste. Mix them very well. Now in a salad bowl add the asparagus, spinach and the dressing and mix. Then add crumbled cooked bacon pieces. Enjoy!

Chili salmon salad

Ingredients

1 salted salmon, diced
1 stalk celery, chopped
½ cup mayonnaise
2 tomatoes, diced

2 green onions, chopped
½ cup fresh sour cream
2 tsp. red chili paste
Fresh lime juice of 1/2 a lemon

Method

Combine all the ingredients in a bowl and toss well till all the ingredients are mixed properly. Refrigerate and serve chilled. Enjoy!

Avocado and grapefruit salad

Ingredients

1 avocado
1 grapefruit
2 cloves of garlic
3-4 dried cranberries
½ cup Mayonnaise

¼ cup fresh sour cream
Drizzle of red wine
Some poppy seeds
Pinch of salt and pepper

Method

Combine all the ingredients in a bowl and toss well till all the ingredients are mixed properly. Refrigerate and serve chilled. Enjoy!

Quinoa with pine nuts

Ingredients

2 cups cooked quinoa
4-5 pine nuts, toasted
Extra virgin olive oil
2 tomatoes, diced

2 tsp. parsley
8-10 mint leaves
Some salt
Pinch of black pepper to taste

Method

Combine all the ingredients in a bowl and toss well till all the ingredients are mixed properly. This salad is best served warm. Enjoy!

Roasted potato salad with curry powder

Ingredients

2-3 Potatoes, diced and roasted
1 tsp. curry power
½ cup mayonnaise
2 tbsp. vinegar
1 stalk celery, chopped
2 tbsp. chopped cilantro

2 scallions, sliced
Salt and pepper, to taste

Method

Combine all the ingredients in a bowl and toss well till all the ingredients are mixed properly. Serve immediately. Enjoy!

Mushroom salad with bulgur and quinoa

Ingredients

1 cup cooked Bulgur
1 cup cooked Quinoa
3-4 mushrooms, chopped

2 peeled tomatoes, diced
Salt
Black or white pepper

Method

Place the tomatoes and mushrooms in a microwave safe bowl and heat for 2-3 minutes. Add in rest of the ingredients and mix well. Serve immediately. Enjoy!

Lemony and Gingery Radish salad

Ingredients

1 radish, boiled and sliced
3 cloves of garlic, minced
1 tsp. cinnamon powder
1 ginger, grated finely

Salt, to taste
Black pepper, to taste
Drizzle of oil

Method

Place the slices of the radish in a plate. Mix the rest of the ingredients to make a dressing. Just before serving pour the dressing over the radish. Enjoy!

Fresh berries and Mango salad

Ingredients

2 mangoes, cubed
2 strawberries, cut into halves
2 cups blueberries
6-8 mint leaves

Salt to taste
Drizzle of Balsamic vinegar
White sugar, to taste

Method

Combine all the ingredients in a bowl and toss well till all the ingredients are mixed properly. Refrigerate and serve chilled. Enjoy!

Simple Bread and feta salad

Ingredients

1 loaf of bread, sliced
1 stalk celery, diced
2 tbsp. lemon juice
Drizzle of olive oil
½ cup Feta cheese

2 Fresh basil leaves
8 Olives
Pinch of salt
Pepper, to taste

Method

First take the bread slices and break into pieces. Add the bread, celery, lemon juice, olive oil, olives, basil leaves, and some salt and if you want, then add some pepper. Add in the Feta cheese and refrigerate. Serve chilled. Enjoy!

Smoky trout salad with Julienned Apples

Ingredients

1 flaked and smoked trout fish
2 tbsp. extra virgin olive oil
1 tsp. horseradish
3 Shallots, minced
1 tsp. Dijon mustard
3 apples, julienned

2 tbsp. vinegar
1 bunch arugula
1 tsp. honey
Pinch of salt
Freshly ground black pepper to taste

Method

Combine all the ingredients in a bowl and toss well till all the ingredients are mixed properly. Serve immediately. Enjoy!

Fava with tomatoes and cucumber salad

Ingredients

1 can fava beans
2 cucumbers, chopped
2 tomatoes, chopped
1 tbsp. parsley
Fresh juice of 1 lemon

1 tbsp. Oil
2 garlic cloves, minced
Pinch of ground cumin
Pinch of salt
Pinch of pepper

Method

Combine all the ingredients in a bowl and toss well till all the ingredients are mixed properly. Serve immediately. Enjoy!

Tasty salad with stale bread

Ingredients

1 packet stale bread
2 tbsp. red wine vinegar
2 cloves of garlic, minced
2 red onions, finely chopped
1 stalk celery, chopped

2 tomatoes, diced
2 tbsp. Olive oil
2-3 Basil leaves
Pinch of salt
Pinch of pepper

Method

Marinate the chunks of tomatoes in olive oil and some vinegar for a few hours. Sprinkle some salt and pepper on it and rest for a while. Soak the stale bread in water and then drain them. In a salad mixing bowl, add the soaked bread and marinated tomatoes along with onions, celery and basil. Serve immediately. Enjoy!

Marinated grated salad

Ingredients

1 head cabbage, grated
2 cucumbers, grated
2 carrots, grated
2 beets, grated
Water, as needed

2 onions, sliced
Drizzle of oil
2 tbsp. vinegar
Salt, to taste

Method

Combine all the ingredients in a bowl and toss well till all the ingredients are mixed properly. Freeze for at least six hours and serve chilled. Enjoy!

Cranberry and walnut salad with blue cheese

Ingredients

5-6 dried cranberries
2-3 Glazed walnuts
2 oranges, segments cut

Salad dressing, according to taste
Blue cheese, crumbled , for garnish
Some fresh basil leaves
Fresh mint

Method

Combine all the ingredients in a bowl and toss well till all the ingredients are mixed properly. Refrigerate and serve chilled. Enjoy!

Garlic shrimp salad with peas

Ingredients

5 Small shrimps, boiled
2 tbsp. extra virgin olive oil
2 Minced cloves of garlic
2 Shallots, minced
1 tsp. Dijon mustard

2 tbsp. Vinegar
1 cup Frozen peas, boiled
Pinch of salt
Freshly ground black pepper to sprinkle

Method

Combine all the ingredients in a bowl and toss well till all the ingredients are mixed properly. Serve immediately. Enjoy!

Fresh Kidney bean salad

Ingredients

1 can of kidney beans
2 cucumbers
2 tomatoes
2 tsp. parsley
Fresh juice of 1 lemon

Oil
2 Cloves of garlic minced
Pinch of ground cumin
Pinch of salt
Pinch of pepper

Method

Now first chop the fresh tomatoes and cucumbers into fine dices. Add the kidney beans to that bowl. Now add the minced cloves of garlic, ground pepper and cumin, pinch of salt to your taste, chopped parsley, drizzle some oil and some fresh lime juice. Toss them very well. Enjoy!

Tortilla and tomato salad

Ingredients

10 Tortillas, into pieces
2 tbsp. Red wine vinegar
2 Minced cloves of garlic
2 red onions
1 stalk celery
3 Tomatoes

Olive oil
Mozzarella, to garnish
Basil leaves, to garnish
Pinch of salt
Pinch of pepper

Method

Firstly you have to cut chunks of tomatoes, drizzle some olive oil and some vinegar. Now sprinkle some salt and some pepper. Keep it as it is for few minutes. Now take the tortillas and break them into pieces. In a salad mixing bowl, add tortilla pieces and marinated tomatoes along with onions, celery and basil. Top with mozzarella and serve. Enjoy!

Red Cabbage and carrot salad

Ingredients

1 head Grated red cabbage
3 Grated carrots
3 Finely sliced onions
Drizzle of oil

2 tbsp. Vinegar
½ cup Mayonnaise
Pinch of sugar
Some milk

Method

First take fresh red cabbage and carrots. Now grate them and put them in a bowl. Now, add some finely sliced onions to this bowl. Now in a separate apparatus, mix the mayonnaise, vinegar, some oil, sugar to taste and some milk. Mix this in the grated vegetables and mix. Keep it in freezer and serve. Enjoy!

Strawberry and pear salad with blue cheese

Ingredients

10-12 sliced strawberries
10 Glazed walnuts
2 Sliced pears
1 bunch Spinach leaves

Salad dressing, according to taste
Blue cheese, crumbled , for garnish
4-5 basil leaves
mint

Method

First cut the strawberries and pears into pieces. Now take salad mixing bowl and add some glazed walnuts and fresh spinach leaves. Now spread the salad dressing and mix them thoroughly. Now add the fresh basil leaves and the fresh mints. Then top the dish with blue cheese, crumbled all over the salad. Have I with bread or with anything you wish. Enjoy!

Tomatoes with mint and basil

Ingredients

4 tomatoes
2 tbsp. Olive oil
2 tbsp. White wine vinegar
Salt to taste

Pepper to taste
mint leaves
2 Shallots, sliced

Method

First cut the fresh tomatoes into chunks. Then take them in a salad mixing bowl. Add some salt, some pepper to taste and the sliced shallots. Keep them for 6 minutes. Now drizzle some white wine vinegar and some extra virgin olive oil. Now top this up with fresh mints. And this simple and tasty salad dish is ready to go with any meal of yours. You may serve this with bread crumbs. Serve topped with mint leaves. Enjoy!

Cranberries with greens

Ingredients

6and trimmed asparagus
1 bunch Baby spinach
½ cup Dried cranberries
Drizzle of olive oil

2 tbsp. Balsamic vinegar to taste
2 cups Salad dressing
Pinch of salt
Ground black pepper

Method

Firstly trim the fresh asparagus and boil them till they become tender. Wash the fresh baby spinach. Now in a small mixing bowl, add some oil, some salad dressing and balsamic vinegar and sprinkle some amount of salt and black ground pepper to taste. Mix them very well. Now in a salad bowl add the asparagus and this mixture and mix. Then add sweet dry cranberries. Enjoy!

Quinoa salad with cranberries and glazed walnuts

Ingredients

2 cups Cooked quinoa
½ cup Dried cranberries
5-6 Glazed walnuts
4 tbsp. Olive oil
4 Well diced tomatoes

2 tbsp. parsley
2 tbsp. mint leaves
Some salt
Pinch of black pepper to taste

Method

Take the cooked quinoa into a deep bowl. Now take the dried cranberries and glazed walnuts in the bowl. Now add the diced fresh tomatoes, some fresh parsley and mint leaves and drizzle some oil. Mix them all well. Now season with salt and black pepper. This tasty dish is ready to go. Enjoy!

Pasta Salad with Salmon

Ingredients

2 pieces Cooked Salmon, diced
1 cup cooked pasta
2 stalks celery
½ cup Mayonnaise
lime juice of 1/2 a lemon

2 diced tomatoes
2-3 freshly chopped green onions
1 cup sour cream
1 Diced Red apple

Method

First take a deep bowl and mix the diced cooked salmon, cooked pasta along with some freshly chopped celery and tomatoes, diced apples and green onions. Mix them well. Now add homemade mayonnaise, fresh sour cream and drizzle fresh lime juice of half a lemon. Now mix them all very thoroughly. This is ready. Enjoy!

Mushroom salad with Spinach and romaine

Ingredients

1 bunch spinach
1 Romaine
4-5 Mushrooms
2 peeled tomatoes
2 tbsp. Butter, optional

Salt
Black or white pepper

Method

Take fresh spinach and romaine. Sauté in butter, optional . It will take hardly 7 to 8 minutes. Meanwhile chop the mushrooms and take in a bowl. Then add tomatoes to the mushrooms. Put this in the microwave for about 2 to 3 minutes. Now mix these with the sautéed spinach and romaine. Mix them well and sprinkle salt and black or white pepper. Enjoy!

Waldorf Salad with Chicken

Ingredients

½ cup of walnuts, chopped
½ cup of honey mustard
3 cups of boiled chicken, chopped
½ cup of mayonnaise
1 cup of red grapes, cut into halves

1 cup of celery, cut into dices
1 Gala apple, cut into dices
Salt
Pepper

Method

Take a shallow pan to bake the chopped walnuts for 7-8 minutes in a pre-heated oven, 350 degrees . Now mix in all the ingredients and adjust the seasoning. Enjoy!

Tangy Potato Arugula Salad

Ingredients

2 pounds of potatoes, cut into cubes and boiled
2 cups of arugula
6 tsp. of extra virgin olive oil
¼ tsp. of black pepper
3 shallots, chopped

3/8 tsp. of salt
½ tsp. of sherry vinegar
1 tsp. of lemon juice
2 tsp. of mustard, grounded in stone
1 tsp. of lemon rind, grated

Method

Heat 1 tsp. of oil in a skillet and sauté shallots till they turn brown. Transfer shallots to a mixing bowl and combine all the remaining ingredients except potatoes. Mix thoroughly. Now top the potatoes with the dressing and give a toss to mix well. Enjoy!

Chicken Salsa with Avocado Salad

Ingredients

2 tsp. of olive oil

4 ounces of tortilla chips

2 tsp. of lime juice

1 avocado, chopped

3/8 tsp. of kosher salt

¾ cup of salsa, cooled

1/8 tsp. of black pepper

2 cups of chicken breast, cooked and shredded

¼ cup of cilantro, chopped

Method

Mix olive oil, lime juice, black pepper and salt in a mixing bowl. Now add chopped cilantro and chicken and mix well. Top with chopped avocado and salsa. Serve the salad on tortilla chips for best results. Enjoy!

Creamy Potato Dill Salad

Ingredients

¾ pound of potatoes, cut in cubes and boiled

¼ tsp. of black pepper

½ of English cucumber, cut into dices

¼ tsp. of kosher salt

2 tsp. of sour cream, low fat

2 tsp. of chopped dill

2 tsp. of yoghurt, fat-free

Method

The potatoes must be boiled till tender. Take a mixing bowl and mix dill, yoghurt, cream, cucumber dices and black pepper. The ingredients should be mixed well. Now add the cooked potato cubes and toss well. Enjoy!

Cheesy Chicken Salad with Arugula Leaves

Ingredients

3 bread slices, cut into cubes

½ cup of Parmesan cheese, shredded

3 tsp. of butter, unsalted and melted

2 tsp. of parsley, chopped

5 basil leaves, cut into strips

¼ cup of olive oil

2 cups of chicken, roasted and chopped

5 ounce of arugula leaves

3 tsp. of red wine vinegar

Pepper, as per taste

Method

Heat butter and 2 tsp. of olive oil and toss the bread cubes in it. Bake the bread cubes in a preheated oven, 400 degrees till it turns golden brown. Add rest of the ingredients with bread cubes and mix well. Enjoy!

Tangy Pepper Potato Salad

Ingredients

2 pounds of Yellow Finn potatoes, cut into cubes
¼ tsp. of white pepper
2 tsp. of salt

¼ cup of cream
4 tsp. of lemon juice
2 sprigs of dill
2 bunches of chives

Method

Boil the potato cubes till tender and drain it. Mix 3 tsp. of lemon juice to the potatoes and keep aside for 30 minutes. Beat the cream till smooth and mix in all the other ingredients. Top the potatoes with the mixture and toss well. Enjoy!

Couscous Chicken Salad

Ingredients

1 cup of couscous
7 ounces of chicken breast, cooked
¼ cup of Kalamata olives, chopped
1 clove of garlic, minced
2 tsp. of parsley, chopped

¼ tsp. of black pepper
1 tsp. of capers, chopped
1 tsp. of lime juice
2 tsp. of olive oil
Salt, to taste

Method

Cook couscous without salt and fat following the package instruction. Rinse the cooked couscous with cold water. Take a mixing bowl to mix the ingredients except chicken and couscous. Add the cooked couscous and mix well. Add the chicken and serve immediately. Enjoy!

Red Potato Salad with Buttermilk

Ingredients

3 pounds of red potatoes, cut in quarters
1 clove of garlic, minced
½ cup of sour cream
½ tsp. of black pepper

1 tsp. of kosher salt
1/3 cup of buttermilk
1 tsp. of dill, chopped
¼ cup of parsley, chopped

2 tsp. of chives, chopped

Method

Boil potato quarters till tender in a Dutch oven. Cool the cooked potatoes for 30-40 minutes. Mix sour cream with rest of the ingredients. Top potatoes with the dressing and give a toss to mix the ingredients. Enjoy!

Chicken Salad with Honeydew Melon

Ingredients

¼ cup of rice vinegar
2 tsp. of walnuts, chopped and toasted
2 tsp. of soy sauce
¼ cup of cilantro, chopped
2 tsp. of peanut butter
2 cups of chicken breast, cooked and grated

1 tsp. of honey
3 tsp. of green onions, sliced
1 cup of cucumber, chopped
¾ tsp. of sesame oil
3 cups of melon, cut into strips
3 cups of cantaloupe, cut into strips

Method

Mix soy sauce, peanut butter, vinegar, honey and sesame oil. Add melon, onions, cantaloupe and cucumber and mix well. Top chicken breast with the mixture and cilantro while serving. Enjoy!

Eggs Potato Salad with Dijon Mustard

Ingredients

4 pounds of potatoes
¾ tsp. of pepper
½ cup of celery, cut into dices
½ cup of parsley, chopped
1 tsp. of Dijon mustard
1/3 cup of green onion, chopped

2 cloves of garlic, chopped
1 tsp. of Dijon mustard
3 eggs, boiled and shredded
½ cup of cream
1 cup of mayonnaise

Method

Cook potatoes till tender. Peel and cut the potatoes into cubes. Mix potatoes, green onion, celery and parsley in a mixing bowl. Mix mayonnaise and other ingredients in a bowl. Top this mixture on potatoes and mix well. Enjoy!

Chicken Salad with Honey and Pecan

Ingredients

4 cups of chicken, cooked and chopped
¼ tsp. of pepper
3 ribs of celery, diced
¼ tsp. of salt

1 cup of sweet cranberries, dried
1/3 cup of honey
½ cup of pecans, chopped and toasted
2 cups of mayonnaise

Method

Mix chopped chicken with celery, dry cranberries and pecans. Whisk mayonnaise till smooth in another bowl. Add honey, pepper and salt to mayonnaise and mix well. Top chicken mixture with mayonnaise mixture and toss well so that the ingredients are mixed well. Enjoy!

Mayo Grape Chicken Salad

Ingredients

6 cups of chicken, chopped and cooked
½ cup of pecans
2 tsp. of Dijon mustard
2 cups of red grapes, sliced
½ cup of sour cream

2 tsp. of poppy seeds
½ cup of mayonnaise
2 cup of celery, chopped
1 tsp. of lemon juice

Method

Take a mixing bowl and mix chicken with mayonnaise, lemon juice, sour cream, grapes, poppy seeds, Dijon mustard and celery. Adjust salt and pepper. Cover the mixing bowl and refrigerate it till chilled. Add pecans and serve immediately. Enjoy!

Cream of Potato Herb Salad

Ingredients

¾ cup of sour cream
1 cup of green peas
¼ cup of yoghurt
6 cups of red potatoes, cut in quarters

1 tsp. of thyme, chopped
½ tsp. of salt
1 tsp. of dill weed, chopped

Method

Mix cream, yoghurt, dill weed, thyme and salt in a mixing bowl and keep it separately.

Cook the potato quarters and green peas in enough water till tender. Drain out the extra water. Mix potato and peas in the mixture prepared. Toss well to mix the ingredients thoroughly. Enjoy!

Tangy Chicken Salad with Raisins

Ingredients

¼ cup of mayonnaise
3 tsp. of raisins
1 tsp. of curry powder
1/3 cup of celery, cut into dices

1 cup of lemon chicken, grilled
1 apple, chopped
1/8 tsp. of salt
2 tsp. of water

Method

Mix curry powder, mayonnaise and water in a bowl. Add lemon chicken, chopped apple, raisins, celery and salt to it. Use a spatula to mix the ingredients thoroughly. Cover the salad and refrigerate till chilled. Enjoy!

Mint Potato Salad

Ingredients

7 red potatoes
1 cup of green peas, frozen and thawed
2 tsp. of white wine vinegar
½ tsp. of black pepper

2 tsp. of olive oil
¾ tsp. of salt
2 tsp. of shallots, finely chopped
¼ cup of mint leaves, chopped

Method

Boil the potatoes in water in a deep bottomed pan till tender. Cool the potatoes and cut into cubes. Mix vinegar, shallots, mint, olive oil, salt and black pepper. Place potato cubes, peas and the mixture prepared. Mix well and serve. Enjoy!

Chicken Curry Salad with Mixed Greens

Ingredients

Chicken curry, frozen and thawed
10 ounce of spinach leaves
1 ½ cups of celery, chopped
¾ cup of mayonnaise
1 ½ cups of green grapes, cut into halves

½ cup of red onions, chopped

Method

In a mixing bowl place the frozen chicken curry. Add red onions, green grapes, baby spinach leaves and celery to the chicken curry. Mix well. Now add in mayonnaise and mix again thoroughly. Adjust the salt and pepper as per taste. Enjoy!

Nutty Chicken Salad

Ingredients

1 cup of bulgur
2 scallions, cut into slices
2 cups of chicken broth
3 cups of chicken, cooked and chopped
1 apple, cut into dices
3 tsp. of walnuts, chopped

¼ cup of olive oil
2 tsp. of cider vinegar
1 tsp. of Dijon mustard
1 tsp. of brown sugar
Salt

Method

Boil bulgur with broth and simmer. Cool for 15 minutes. Toast walnuts in a frying pan and place in a bowl to cool. In a mixing bowl mix all the ingredients thoroughly. Adjust salt and serve. Enjoy!

Mustard Chicken Salad

Ingredients

1 egg, boiled
¼ tsp. of black pepper
¾ pound of fingerling potatoes
¼ tsp. of kosher salt
2 tsp. of mayonnaise, low fat

3 tsp. of red onion, chopped
1 tsp. of yoghurt
1/3 cup of celery, chopped
1 tsp. of mustard

Method

Cut potatoes into cubes and boil till tender. Chop the boiled egg. Mix all the ingredients except eggs and potatoes. Add the mixture on the chopped eggs and potato cubes. Toss well so that the ingredients mix well. Adjust salt and pepper as per taste. Enjoy!

Tangy Ginger Potato Salad

Ingredients

2 pounds of red potatoes, cut into cubes
2 tsp. of cilantro, chopped
2 tsp. of rice vinegar
1/3 cup of green onion, sliced
1 tsp. sesame oil

1 jalapeno pepper, finely chopped
4 tsp. of lemongrass, minced
¾ tsp. of salt
2 tsp. of ginger, grated

Method

Boil potatoes till they turn tender. Drain out the excess water. Combine rest of the ingredients thoroughly. Top the boiled potatoes with the mixture. Use a spatula to mix the ingredients. Enjoy!

Celery and Potato Salad

Ingredients

2 pounds of red potatoes, cut into cubes
2 ounce of pimientos, diced
½ cup of canola mayonnaise
1/8 tsp. of garlic powder
¼ cup of green onions, chopped
¼ tsp. of black pepper
¼ cup of yogurt

½ tsp. of celery seeds
¼ cup of cream, sour
½ tsp. of salt
1 tsp. of sugar
1 tsp. of white wine vinegar
2 tsp. of prepared mustard

Method

Boil potato cubes till they turn tender and drain out the excess water. Cool the boiled potatoes for about 30 minutes. Mix rest of the ingredients in a mixing bowl. Add potato cubes and toss well to mix. Enjoy!

Lime Chicken with Potato Salad

Ingredients

1 pound of potatoes
1 clove of garlic, chopped
2 cups of peas
½ tsp. of black pepper
2 cups of chicken breast, chopped

1 tsp. of salt
½ cup of red bell pepper, chopped
1 tsp. of salt
½ cup of onion, chopped
1 tsp. of tarragon, minced

1 tsp. of lime juice
2 tsp. of olive oil

1 tsp. of Dijon mustard

Method

Cook potato, peas and chicken breast separately till tender. Mix rest of the ingredients in a bowl. Now add potato cubes, peas and chicken breast in the mixing bowl. Use a spatula and mix the ingredients thoroughly. Serve immediately. Enjoy!

Potato Salad with Goat Cheese

Ingredients

2 ½ pounds of potatoes
1 clove of garlic, minced
¼ cup of white wine, dry
1 tsp. of Dijon mustard
½ tsp. of salt
2 tsp. of olive oil
½ tsp. of black pepper

2 tsp. of tarragon, chopped
1/3 cup of onion, chopped
¼ cup of red wine vinegar
½ cup of parsley, chopped
3 ounce of goat cheese
¼ cup of sour cream

Method

Boil potatoes in water till tender. Mix potatoes, wine vinegar, pepper and salt in a bowl. Keep aside for 15 minutes. Now add rest of the ingredients to the potato mixture and mix well. Serve immediately. Enjoy!

Pico de Gallo - Authentic Mexican Salsa

Ingredients:

3 large Diced tomatoes, sautéed
1 diced Medium sized onion
¼ bunch Cilantro, use more or less depending on your taste
Optional ingredients
½ Peeled and diced cucumber

Lemon juice of ½ lemon
½ tsp. Minced garlic
Salt to taste
2 Jalapenos, or more if you prefer it hotter
1 dice Peeled avocado

Method

Combine all the ingredients in a large mixing bowl and toss well. Serve immediately. Enjoy!

Olive Oil and Lemon Salad Dressing

Ingredients:

8 cloves of garlic minced
½ tsp. Black pepper
1 cup Freshly squeezed lemon juice

2 tsp. Salt
½ cup Extra Virgin Olive Oil

Method

Place all the ingredients in a blender and blend until all the ingredients are incorporated. This dressing should be stored in an air tight container and should be used soon, or else the dressing will get bitter due to the lemon juice in it. Enjoy!

Bean, Corn & Avocado Salad

Ingredients:

1 can black Beans, drained
1 can Yellow Sweet Corn, Canned , drained
2 tbsp. Lime Juice
1 tsp. Olive Oil

4 tbsp. Cilantro
5 cups chopped raw onions
1 Avocado
1 Red Ripe Tomatoes

Method

Place all the ingredients in a large mixing bowl and mix gently. Serve immediately or serve cold. Enjoy!

Southwest Pasta Salad

Ingredients:

1-8 ounces Small whole-wheat pasta
15 ounces Corn
15 ounces Black beans

1 cup Salsa, any variety
1 cup cheddar cheese, shredded
1 cup Diced green pepper, bell pepper

Method

Prepare pasta according to package directions. Drain, rinse and put into large bowl. The liquids are reserved and drained from the canned corn and black beans. Combine all ingredients with the cooked pasta in a large bowl. Add small amounts of the reserved canned liquids are added if required. Serve immediately. Enjoy!

Roasted Beet Salad

Ingredients:

6 Yellow beets, 1/2 pound
3 tbsp. Olive oil
Fresh cracked black pepper
1 ½ tbsp. Tarragon or sherry vinegar

1 tbsp. thyme leaves
4 cups Mixed salad greens
½ cup Crumbled feta cheese
1 tbsp. mint

Method

At first the oven is pre heated to 375 degrees. Place the beets in a shallow covered baking dish. Add enough water to come 1/2 inch up the dish. Cover the beets and roast for an hour or until beets are easily pierced by a paring knife. Remove the beets from the oven. In a medium bowl, whisk together the vinegar and chopped herbs. Chop the cooked beets into 1/2 inch cubes, and then toss with the dressing. Sprinkle on the feta cheese and serve immediately. Enjoy!

Oh Boy, Salad!

Ingredients:

1 cup Tomatoes, chopped or sliced
1 cup Pared cucumber, chopped

1 tsp. Dried dill weed
1 tbsp. Light mayonnaise

Method

Add all the ingredients in a large bowl and toss well until all the ingredients are incorporated. Refrigerate overnight and serve chilled. Enjoy!!

Crunchy Cabbage Ramen Noodle Salad

Ingredients:

3 tbsp. Olive oil
3 tbsp. Vinegar
2 tbsp. Sugar, or sugar substitute
½ package Ramen noodle seasoning
¼ tsp. Pepper
1 tbsp. Low sodium soy sauce

Ingredients for salad:
1 small head Red or green cabbage
2 Chopped green onions, chopped
1 Peeled carrot and grated
1 package Crushed ramen noodle

Method

Make the dressing by combining the ingredients in a large salad mixing bowl. Stir to dissolve sugar. The first three salad ingredients are added to a bowl and tossed well. Add in the crushed Ramen and mix well. Pour the dressing over and serve immediately. Enjoy!

Spinach and Tomato Pasta Salad

Ingredients:

8oz. Small pasta or orzo
8 oz. Crumbled feta cheese
16 oz. Grape tomatoes
4 cups Baby Spinach

2 tbsp. Drained capers
¼ tsp. Black pepper
2 tbsp. Shredded Parmesan cheese

Method

Cook pasta according to package directions until it is al dente, firm to bite . Once pasta is cooked; drain it over the tomatoes for a quick blanch. While the pasta is cooking, the spinach, feta, and capers are to be placed in a large bowl. Toss tomatoes and pasta with the spinach mixture. Before draining pasta, the pasta cooking is proportionately added to combine. Finally season it with black pepper and garnish with shredded cheese. Serve immediately. Enjoy!

Waldorf Salad

Ingredients:

4 Medium apples, cubed
1/3 cup chopped walnuts
1/3 cup Raisins

½ cup Low-fat plain yogurt, Greek or regular
3 stalks Chopped celery

Method

Add all the ingredients in a large bowl and toss well until all the ingredients are incorporated. Refrigerate overnight and serve chilled. Enjoy!

Istuaeli Salad

Ingredients:

1 Green or yellow bell pepper, chopped
1 Peeled Cucumber, chopped
2 tbsp. Lemon juice
1 tsp. Salt

1 tsp. Fresh ground pepper
3 Tomatoes, chopped
3 tbsp. extra virgin olive oil

Method

Add all the ingredients in a large bowl and toss well until all the ingredients are incorporated. Serve immediately as the more this salad sits, the watery it gets. Enjoy!

Cabbage Noodle Salad

Ingredients:

3 tbsp. Olive oil3 tbsp. Vinegar2 tbsp. Sugar½ package Ramen noodle
¼ tsp. Pepper
1 tbsp. Low sodium soy sauce

1 Head red or green cabbage
2 Green onions, chopped
1Peeled carrot, grated
1 package Crushed ramen noodles

Method

All ingredients are combined in a large bowl. Keep stirring properly to dissolve sugar. Then the first three salient ingredients of this salad are combined then all are tossed well. Crushed ramen noodles are added to it. Then the rest of the ingredients are added to it then toss it repeatedly. Serve right away or cover and refrigerate to allow the flavors to blend. Enjoy!

Mexican Black Bean Salad

Ingredients

1 ½ can cooked black beans
2 Ripe plum tomatoes, diced
3 Scallions, sliced
1 tbsp. Fresh lime juice
2 tbsp. freshly chopped cilantro

Salt and freshly ground black pepper to taste
1/3 cup corn
2 tbsp. Olive oil

Method

Combine all ingredients in a medium size bowl and toss gently. Let the salad rest in the refrigerator until serving time. Serve chilled. Enjoy!

Black Bean and Corn Salsa

Ingredients:

1 can Black beans
3 tbsp. freshly chopped cilantro
1 can Yellow corn and white corn

¼ cup Chopped onion
1 can Rootle
Lime juice, or squeeze one lime

Method

Drain the liquid from the black beans, rootle and corn cans and combine them in a large bowl. Add in the cilantro and onion and mix well. Just before serving, squeeze in some lemon juice. Enjoy!

Turkey Taco Salad

Ingredients:

2 oz. Ground turkey
2/4 cup Cheddar cheese
1 ½ cups Romaine lettuce, chopped
1/8 cup Onions, chopped

½ oz. Tortilla chips
2 tbsp. Salsa
¼ cup Red kidney beans

Method

Add all the ingredients in a large bowl except for the tortilla chips and toss well. Just before serving, top the salad with the crushed tortillas and serve immediately. Enjoy!

Rainbow Fruit Salad

Ingredients

Fruit salad:
1 large Peeled mango, diced
2 cups blueberries
2 Sliced bananas
2 cups strawberries
2 cups Seedless grapes
2 tbsp. Lemon juice
1 ½ tbsp. Honey

2 cups Seedless grapes
2 Unpeeled nectarines, sliced
1 Peeled kiwi fruit, sliced
Honey orange sauce:
1/3 cup Unsweetened orange juice
¼ tsp. Ground ginger
Dash nutmeg

Method

Add all the ingredients in a large bowl and toss well until all the ingredients are incorporated. Refrigerate overnight and serve chilled. Enjoy!

Sunshine Fruit Salad

Ingredients:

3 Kiwis, sliced into bite sized pieces
320 oz. Pineapple chunks in juice

215 oz. Drained mandarin oranges, canned in light syrup

2 Bananas

Method

Combine all the ingredients in a large mixing bowl and refrigerate for at least 2 hours. Serve this salad chilled. Enjoy!

Citrus and Black Bean Salad

Ingredients:

1 Peeled grapefruit, sectioned
2 Peeled oranges, sectioned
116oz. Drained can of black beans
½ cup Red onion chopped

½ Sliced avocado
2 tbsp. Lemon juice
Black pepper to taste

Method

Combine all the ingredients in a large mixing bowl and serve at room temperature. Enjoy!

Tangy Cucumber and Onion Salad

Ingredients

2 Cucumbers, thinly sliced
½ tsp. Salt
¼ tsp. Black pepper
2 tbsp. Granulated sugar

1/3 cup Cider vinegar
1 Onion, thinly sliced
1/3 cup Water

Method

Layer the cucumbers and onions alternatingly in a dish. Combine the rest of the ingredients in a blender and blend until smooth. Chill the dressing for a few hours. Just before serving, spoon the dressing over the cucumbers and onions and serve immediately. Enjoy!

Garden Salad with Blueberries and Beets

Ingredients:

1 head Romaine lettuce
1 handful blueberries
1 oz. goat cheese Crumbled

2 Roasted beets
5-6 Cherry tomatoes ¼ cup Canned tuna
Salt, to taste

Pepper, to taste

Method

Place all the ingredients in a greased baking dish and cover with a foil. Bake in a preheated oven at 250 degrees F for an hour or so. Cool a bit and season per your taste. Serve hot. Enjoy!

Cauliflower or Mock Potato Salad

Ingredients

1 Head cauliflower, boiled and cut into florets
¼ cup Fat free milk
6 tsp. Splenda

¾ tbsp. Cider vinegar
5 tbsp. Light mayonnaise
2 tsp. Yellow mustard

Method

Combine all the ingredients except for the cauliflower and whisk until smooth. Just before serving top the boiled cauliflower with the prepared dressing and serve warm. Enjoy!

Cucumber Dill Salad

Ingredients:

1 cup Non-Fat Greek Yogurt or Fat free plain
Salt and Pepper to taste
6 cups cucumber, thinly sliced

½ cup Onion, thinly sliced
¼ cup Lemon juice
2 cloves Minced Garlic
1/8 cup Dill weed

Method

Drain the excess water from the yoghurt and chill for about 30 minutes. Combine the yoghurt with rest of the ingredients and mix well. Refrigerate for another hour or so and serve chilled. Enjoy!

Faux Potato Salad

Ingredients

16 tbsp. Fat free mayonnaise
5 cups boiled cauliflower, cut into florets

¼ cup Yellow mustard
¼ cup Chopped celery

½ cup Sliced cucumber
1 tbsp. Yellow mustard seed

¼ cup Dill pickles diced
½ tsp. Garlic powder

Method

Add all the ingredients in a large bowl and toss well until all the ingredients are incorporated. Refrigerate overnight and serve chilled. You can even substitute the cauliflower for potatoes, the dish tastes equally delicious. Enjoy!

Bonnie Auntie's Potato Cucumber Salad

Ingredients

2-3 cups New potatoes
1 tbsp. Cube dill
1 tbsp. Dijon mustard
¼ cup Flax oil
4 chives, chopped

2 tsp. dill, chopped
¼ tsp. Pepper
3-4 cups Cucumber
¼ tsp. Salt

Method

Combine all the ingredients in a large bowl and toss well until all the ingredients are incorporated, just before serving. Serve immediately. Enjoy!

Berry-Good Spinach Salad

Ingredients

½ cup Sliced strawberries
¼ cup raspberries
¼ cup Newman›s Own Light Raspberry and Walnut Dressing

¼ cup blueberries
¼ cup Slivered almonds
4 cup spinach
¼ cup Red onions chopped

Method

Add all the ingredients in a large bowl and toss well until all the ingredients are incorporated. Refrigerate overnight and serve chilled. Enjoy!

Tubule Salad

Ingredients

1 cup Bulgur wheat
1 Chopped onion

4 Scallions, minced
Salt and pepper to taste

2 cups Minced Parsley leaf
¼ cup lemon juice
2 cups Boiling water

2 Medium tomatoes, diced
¼ cup Olive oil
1 cup minced mint

Method

In a medium sauce pan, boil water. After removing from heat, pour in the bugler and cover with tight fitting lid and keep aside for 30 minutes. Drain the excess water. Add the remaining ingredients and mix well. Serve immediately. Enjoy!

B.L.T. Salad with Basil Mayo Dressing

Ingredients

½ pound Bacon
½ cup Mayonnaise
2 tbsp. Red wine vinegar
¼ cup Finely chopped basil
1 tsp. pepper Ground black

1 tbsp. Canola oil
1 pound Romaine lettuce - rinsed, dried, and torn into bite-size pieces
¼ pint Cherry tomatoes

Method

Place bacon in a large, deep skillet. Cook over medium high heat until it is evenly brown. In a small bowl add the reserved bacon dripping, mayonnaise, basil and vinegar and whisk together. Cover and keep aside at room temperature. In a large bowl mix together the romaine, bacons and croutons, tomatoes. Pour the dressing over the salad. Serve. Enjoy!

Knife and Fork Grilled Caesar Salad

Ingredients

1 Long thin baguette
¼ cup Olive oil, divided
2 Garlic, halved
1 Small tomato
1 Romaine lettuce, outer leaves discarded

Salt and coarsely black ground pepper to taste
1 cup Caesar salad dressing, or to taste
½ cup Parmesan cheese shaving

Method

Preheat grill on low heat and lightly oil the grate. Cut baguette to make 4 long slices about 1/2-inch thick. Lightly brush each cut side with about half of the olive oil. Grill baguette slices on the preheated grill until lightly crispy, 2 to 3 minutes per side. Rub each side of baguette slices with the cut-side of garlic and cut-side of tomatoes. Brush

2 cut sides of romaine quarters with remaining olive oil. Drizzle each with Caesar dressing. Enjoy!

Strawberry Romaine Salad I

Ingredients:

1 Head lettuce romaine, rinsed, dried, and chopped
2 Bunches washed spinach, dried and chopped
2 Pint strawberries, sliced
1 Bermuda onion

½ cup Mayonnaise
2 tbsp. White wine vinegar
1/3 cup White sugar
¼ cup Milk
2 tbsp. Poppy seeds

Method

In a large salad bowl, combine the romaine, spinach, strawberries and sliced onion. In a jar with a tight fitting lid, combine the mayonnaise, vinegar, sugar, milk and poppy seeds. Shake well and pour the dressing over salad. Toss until evenly coated. Serve immediately. Enjoy!

Greek Salad

Ingredients:

1 Romaine dried lettuce
6 ounce olives Pitted black
1 Green bell pepper, chopped
1 thinly sliced Red onion
6 tbsp. Olive oil
1 Red bell pepper, chopped

2 Large tomatoes, chopped
1 Cucumber, sliced
1 cup Crumbled feta cheese
1 tsp. Dried oregano
1 Lemon

Method

In a large mixing salad bowl, the Romaine, onion, olives, bell peppers, cucumber, tomatoes, and cheese are well mixed. Whisk together the olive oil, lemon juice, oregano, and black pepper. Pour dressing over salad, toss and serve. Enjoy!

Strawberry and Feta Salad

Ingredients

1 cup Slivered almonds

2 cloves Garlic minced

1 tsp. Honey1 cup Vegetable oil
1 Head romaine lettuce,
1 tsp. Dijon mustard
¼ cup Raspberry vinegar

2 tbsp. Balsamic vinegar
2 tbsp. Brown sugar
1 Pint strawberries, sliced
1 cup Crumbled feta cheese

Method

In a skillet the oil is heated over medium-high, cook the almonds, stirring frequently, until lightly toasted. Remove from heat. In a bowl, prepare the dressing by combining the Balsamic vinegar, brown sugar, and vegetable oil together. In a big bowl, mix together the almonds, feta cheese and romaine lettuce. Just before serving toss the salad with the dressing. Enjoy!

Steak Salad

Ingredients

1 ¾ pound Sirloin steak
1/3 cup Olive oil
3 tbsp. Red wine vinegar
2 tbsp. Lemon juice
1 clove Garlic, minced
½ tsp. Salt

1/8 tsp. Ground black pepper
1 tsp. Worcestershire sauce
1 Carrot, sliced
½ cup Sliced red onion
¼ cup Stuffed green sliced pimento olives

Method

Preheat grill on high heat. Place steak on grill and cook for 5 minutes per side. Remove from heat and let sit until cool. In a small bowl, whisk together the olive oil, vinegar, lemon juice, garlic, salt, pepper and Worcestershire sauce. Mix in the cheese. After that, cover and place dressing in refrigerator. Just before serving pour the dressing over the steak. Serve with crusty grilled French bread. Enjoy!

Mandarin Almond Salad

Ingredients:

1 Romaine lettuce
11 ounces Mandarin oranges, drained
6 Green onions, thinly sliced
½ cup Olive oil1 tbsp. White sugar
1 tsp. Crushed red pepper flakes
2 tbsp. White sugar
½ cup Sliced almonds

¼ cup Red wine vinegar
Ground black pepper to taste

Method

In a large bowl, combine the romaine lettuce, oranges and green onions. In a skillet add the sugar and stir while sugar starts to melt. Stir constantly. Add almonds and stir until coated. Turn the almonds onto a plate, and cool. Combine olive oil, red wine vinegar, one tbsp. sugar, pepper red flakes and black pepper in a jar with a tight fitting lid. Before serving, toss lettuce with salad dressing until coated. Transfer to a serving bowl, and serve sprinkled with sugared almonds. Serve immediately. Enjoy!

Tropical Salad with Pineapple Vinaigrette

Ingredients

6 Bacon slices
¼ cup Pineapple juice
3 tbsp. Red wine vinegar
¼ cup Olive oil
Freshly ground black pepper to taste
Salt to taste
10 ounces Package chopped romaine

lettuce
1 cup Diced pineapple
½ cup Chopped and toasted macadamia nuts
3 Chopped green onions
¼ cup Flaked coconut toasted

Method

Place bacon in a large, deep skillet. Cook over medium-high heat until evenly browned, about 10 minutes. Drain and crumble the bacon. Combine pineapple juice, red wine vinegar, oil, pepper and salt in a lidded jar. Cover to shake well. Toss the rest of the ingredients together and add in the dressing. Garnish with toasted coconut. Serve immediately. Enjoy!

California Salad Bowl

Ingredients:

1 Avocado, peeled and pitted
1 tbsp. Lemon juice
½ cup Mayonnaise
¼ tsp. Hot pepper sauce
¼ cup Olive oil
1 clove Garlic, minced
½ tsp. Salt

1 Head romaine lettuce
3 ounces Cheddar cheese, shredded
2 Diced tomatoes
2 Green chopped onions
¼ can pitted green olives
1 cup coarsely crushed corn chips

Method

In a blender, mix all lemon juice, components avocado, mayonnaise, olive oil, hot pepper sauce, garlic, and salt. Until it is smooth keep processing. In a large bowl, mix together the Cheddar cheese, romaine lettuce, tomatoes and avocado and top with the dressing just before serving. Enjoy!

Classic Tossed Salad

Ingredients:

1 cup Blanched slivered almonds
2 tbsp. Sesame seeds
1 Romaine lettuce, torn into bite-size pieces
1 Red leaf lettuce, torn into bite-size pieces
8 ounces Package crumbled feta cheese

4 ounces Can sliced black olives
1 cup Cherry tomatoes, halved
1 Red onion, halved and thinly sliced
6 mushrooms, sliced
¼ cup Grated Romano cheese
8 ounces Bottle Italian salad dressing

Method

Heat a large skillet over medium-high heat. Place the almonds in the skillet, and cook. When the almonds start releasing an aroma, add in the sesame seeds, stirring frequently. Cook for 1 more minute or until seeds are toasted. In a big salad bowl, mix lettuce with olives, feta cheese, mushrooms, almonds, tomatoes, sesame seeds, onion, and Romano cheese are properly combined. When ready to serve, Pour in the Italian dressing and toss. Enjoy!

Fatoosh

Ingredients:

Change Servings
2 Pita breads
8 Leaves romaine lettuce, torn into bite-size pieces
2 Green onions, chopped
1 Cucumber, chopped
3 Tomatoes cut into wedges

1 clove Garlic, peeled and chopped
2 tbsp. Sumac powder
¼ cup Lemon juice
¼ cup Olive oil
1 tsp. Salt
¼ tsp. Ground black pepper
¼ cup Chopped mint leaves

Method

Preheat oven to 350 degrees F, 175 degrees C . Toast pitas for 5 to 10 minutes in the preheated oven, until crisp. Break into bite size pieces. In a large bowl, mix together pita toasted pieces, and green onions, romaine lettuce, cucumber, and tomatoes. Serve immediately. Enjoy!

Tangy Pear and Blue Cheese Salad

Ingredients

1/3 cup ketchup
½ cup distilled white vinegar
¾ cup white sugar
2 tsp. Salt
1 cup canola oil

2 heads romaine lettuce, chopped
4 ounces Crumbled blue cheese
2 Pears, Peeled, cored and chopped
½ cup Toasted chopped walnuts
½ Red onion, chopped

Method

In a small bowl, ketchup, sugar, vinegar, and salt are well combined. Gradually pour in oil, stirring constantly, until well blended. In a large serving bowl, toss together the lettuce, blue cheese, pears, walnuts, and red onion. Pour dressing over salad and toss to coat. Enjoy!

Spicy Italian Salad

Ingredients:

½ cup Canola oil
1/3 cup Tarragon vinegar
1 tbsp. White sugar
1 Red bell pepper, cut into strips
1 Grated carrot
1 Thinly sliced red onion

¼ cup Black olives
¼ cup Pitted green olives
½ cup Sliced cucumber
2 tbsp. Grated Romano cheese
Ground black pepper to taste

Method

In a medium container mix the canola oil, sugar, dry mustard, thyme and garlic in a bowl. In a large bowl, toss together lettuce, red bell pepper, carrot, red onion, artichoke hearts, black olives, green olives, cucumber, and Romano cheese. Place in the refrigerator for 4 hours, or overnight. Season with pepper and salt. Serve chilled. Enjoy!

Caesar Salad II

Ingredients:

1 head romaine lettuce
2 cups Croutons
1 Juiced lemon

1 Dash Worcestershire sauce
6 cloves garlic, minced
1 tbsp. Dijon mustard

½ cup Olive oil   ¼ cup Parmesan Grated cheese

Method

Crush the croutons in a deep mixing bowl .Set aside. Mix the mustard, lemon juice and Worcestershire sauce in a bowl. Blend thoroughly in a mixer and slowly add olive oil until creamy. Pour dressing over the lettuce. Add the croutons and cheese and toss well. Serve immediately. Enjoy!

Salad with Prosciutto and Caramelized Pears and Walnuts

Ingredients:

2 cups orange juice   ¼ cup Water
2 tbsp. Red wine vinegar   ¾ cup virgin Extra olive oil
2 tbsp. finely chopped red onion   1 tbsp. Butter
1 tbsp. White sugar   2 Pears - peeled, cored and cut into
1 tbsp. White wine   wedges
1 cup Walnut halves   Prosciutto, cut into thin strips-1/4 pound
½ cup White sugar   2 Romaine hearts, rinsed and torn

Method

In a medium saucepan, first heat orange juice over medium-high heat, whisking often, until it is reduced by 1/4. Add to a blender, along with the vinegar, onion, sugar, wine, salt and pepper. Melt butter in a non-stick skillet over medium heat while blending on a low speed, remove cap and slowly drizzle in the olive oil to emulsify the dressing. Add sugar and water and cook, stirring constantly. Sauté pears and nuts in butter for 3 minutes. Remove from heat and set aside to cool. Add vinaigrette. Now, serve on a large Italian platter. Enjoy!

Romaine and Mandarin Orange Salad with Poppy Seed Dressing

Ingredients:

6 Slices bacon   10 ounces Mandarin drained orange
1/3 cup Apple cider vinegar   segments
¾ cup White sugar   ¼ cup Toasted slivered almonds
½ cup Red coarsely chopped onion
½ tsp. Dry mustard powder
¼ tsp. Salt
½ cup Vegetable oil1 tsp. Poppy seeds
10 cups Torn romaine lettuce leaves

Method

Brown the bacon in a skillet. Drain, crumble and set aside. Place vinegar, sugar, red onion, mustard powder, and salt into the bowl of a blender. Reduce blender speed to medium-low. Stir in the poppy seeds, now blend until incorporated and the dressing is creamy. Toss the romaine with the crumbled bacon and Mandarin oranges in a large bowl. Top with the dressing and serve immediately. Enjoy!

House Salad Restaurant-Style

Ingredients:

Change Servings
1 Romaine Large head lettuce- rinsed, dried and torn into pieces
4 ounces Jar pimento diced peppers, drained
2/3 cup Extra virgin olive oil
1/3 cup Red wine vinegar
1 tsp. Salt

1 Large head iceberg - rinsed, dried and torn into pieces
14 ounces Artichoke hearts, drained and quartered
1 cup Sliced red onion
¼ tsp. Ground black pepper
2/3 cup cheese - grated Parmesan

Method

Combine all the ingredients in a bowl and toss well. Serve immediately. Enjoy!

Spinach Salad

Ingredients:

Change Servings
½ cup White sugar
1 cup Vegetable oil
2 tbsp. Worcestershire sauce
1/3 cup Ketchup
½ cup White vinegar

1 Small chopped onion
1 pound spinach - rinsed, dried and torn into bite size pieces
4 ounces Sliced water drained chestnuts
5 Slices bacon

Method

Combine all the ingredients in a bowl and toss well. Serve immediately. Enjoy!

Super Seven Spinach Salad

Ingredients:

6 ounces Package baby spinach leaves
1/3 cup Cubed Cheddar cheese
1 Peeled, cored and diced Fuji apple
1/3 cup Finely chopped red onion

¼ cup Sweetened dried cranberries
1/3 cup Blanched slivered almonds
3 tbsp. Poppy seed salad dressing

Method

Combine all the ingredients in a bowl and toss well. Serve immediately. Enjoy!

Beautiful Salad

Ingredients:

8 cups Baby spinach leaves
11 ounces Can mandarin drained oranges
½ Medium red onion, separately sliced
into rings

1 cup feta Crumbled cheese
1 cup vinaigrette Balsamic salad dressing
1 ½ cups Sweetened dried cranberries
1 cup Honey-roasted sliced almonds

Method

Combine all the ingredients in a bowl and toss well. Serve immediately. Enjoy!

Spinach and Orzo Salad

Ingredients:

16 ounces Package uncooked orzo pasta
10 ounces Package finely chopped baby
spinach leaves
½ pound Crumbled feta cheese
½ Red nicely chopped onion

¾ cup Pine nuts
½ tsp. Dried basil
¼ tsp. Ground white pepper
½ cup Olive oil
½ cup Balsamic vinegar

Method

Bring a large pot of lightly salted water to a boil. Transfer to a large bowl and stir in spinach, feta, onion, pine nuts, basil and white pepper. Add orzo and cook for 8 to 10 minutes, drain and rinse with cold water. Toss with olive oil and balsamic vinegar. Refrigerate and serve cold. Enjoy!

Strawberry, Kiwi, and Spinach Salad

Ingredients:

2 tbsp. Raspberry vinegar
2 ½ tbsp. Raspberry jam
1/3 cup Vegetable oil
8 cups Spinach, rinsed and torn into bite-

size pieces
½ cup Chopped walnuts
8 Quartered strawberries
2 Peeled and sliced kiwis

Method

Combine all the ingredients in a bowl and toss well. Serve immediately. Enjoy!

Spinach Pomegranate Salad

Ingredients:

1, 10 ounce bag baby spinach leaves,
rinsed and drained
1/4 red onion, sliced very thin
1/2 cup walnut pieces
1/2 cup crumbled feta

1/4 cup alfalfa sprouts, optional
1 pomegranate, peeled and seeds
separated
4 tbsp. balsamic vinaigrette

Method

Place spinach in a salad bowl. Top with red onion, walnuts, feta, and sprouts. Sprinkle pomegranate seeds over the top, and drizzle with vinaigrette. Enjoy!

Spinach Salad with Pepper Jelly Dressing

Ingredients1

pepper jelly
2 tbsp. Olive oil
1/8 tsp. Salt

2 cups Baby spinach leaves
2 ounces Sliced goat cheese
1/8 tsp. Dijon mustard

Method

Combine all the ingredients in a bowl and toss well. Serve immediately. Enjoy!

Super Easy Spinach and Red Pepper Salad

Ingredients:

¼ cup Olive oil
6 ounces Package baby spinach
½ cup cheese - grated Parmesan

¼ cup Rice vinegar
1 Red bell chopped pepper

Method

Combine all the ingredients in a bowl and toss well. Serve immediately. Enjoy!

Spinach Watermelon-Mint Salad

Ingredients:

1 tbsp. Poppy seeds
¼ cup White sugar10 ounces Bag baby spinach leaves
1 cup Apple cider vinegar
¼ cup Worcestershire sauce
½ cup Vegetable oil

1 tbsp. Sesame seeds
2 cups Cubed seeded watermelon
1 cup Finely chopped mint leaves
1 Small thinly sliced red onion
1 cup Chopped toasted pecans

Method

Combine all the ingredients in a bowl and toss well. Serve immediately. Enjoy!

Pretty Pomegranate Salad

Ingredients:

10 ounces Can drained mandarin oranges
10 ounces baby spinach leaves
10 ounces Arugula leaves

1 Peeled pomegranate and seeds separated
½ Red thinly sliced onion

Method

Combine all the ingredients in a bowl and toss well. Serve immediately. Enjoy!

Apple Almond Crunch Salad

Ingredients:

10 ounces Package mixed salad greens

½ cup Slivered almonds

½ cup Crumbled feta cheese
1 cup Tart chopped and cored apple
¼ cup Sliced red onion

¼ cup Golden raisins
1 cup Raspberry vinaigrette salad dressing

Method

Combine all the ingredients in a bowl and toss well. Serve immediately. Enjoy!

Mandarin Orange, Gorgonzola and Almond Delight

Ingredients:

½ cup Blanched slivered almonds, dry roasted
1 cup Gorgonzola cheese
2 tbsp. Red wine vinegar

11 ounces Mandarin oranges, juice reserved
2 tbsp. Vegetable oil
12 ounces mixed salad greens

Method

Combine all the ingredients in a bowl and toss well. Serve immediately. Enjoy!

Tossed Romaine and Orange Salad

Ingredients:

½ cup Orange juice
1 romaine large head lettuce - torn, washed and dried
3 cans Mandarin oranges
½ cup Slivered almonds

3 tbsp. Olive oil
2 tbsp. Red wine vinegar
½ tsp. Ground black pepper
¼ tsp. Salt

Method

Combine all the ingredients in a bowl and toss well. Serve immediately. Enjoy!

That Addicting Salad

Ingredients:

1 cup Mayonnaise
½ cup freshly grated cheese
½ cup Grated carrot
¼ cup freshly cheese - grated Parmesan
2 tbsp. White sugar

10 ounces Package spring lettuce mix
½ cup Small cauliflower florets
½ cup Bacon bits

Method

In a small bowl, 1/4 cup Parmesan cheese, and sugar, mayonnaise are combined together until they are properly blended. Cover, then keep it to refrigerate overnight. Combine the lettuce, bacon bits, 1/2 cup carrot, Parmesan cheese, cauliflower in a large serving bowl. Mix with chilled dressing just before serving. Enjoy!

Kale Salad with Pomegranate, Sunflower Seeds and Sliced Almonds

Ingredients:

½ pound Kale
1 ½ cups Pomegranate seeds
5 tbsp. Balsamic vinegar
3 tbsp. extra virgin olive oil

2 tbsp. Sunflower seeds
1/3 cup Slivered almonds
5 tbsp. Red pepper seasoned rice vinegar
Salt to taste

Method

Wash and shake off extra water from the kale. Chop the leaves until fine but still a little leafy. The sliced almonds, chopped kale, pomegranate seeds, and sunflower seeds are mixed in a large bowl; toss to combine. Remove the center ribs and stems. The olive oil, rice vinegar, balsamic vinegar mixture is sprayed over the kale mixture and tossed. It is seasoned with salt to serve. Enjoy!

Pomegranate Feta Salad with Lemon Dijon Vinaigrette

Ingredients:

10 ounces Package mixed baby greens
8 ounces Package crumbled feta cheese
1 Zested and juiced lemon
1 tsp. Dijon mustard
Salt and pepper to taste

1 Peeled pomegranate and seeds separated
3 tbsp. Red wine vinegar
3 tbsp. Extra-virgin olive oil

Method

The lettuce, feta cheese, and pomegranate seeds are placed into a large mixing bowl. Then, the lemon juice and zest, vinegar, mustard, salt, olive oil and pepper are whisked together in a large separate bowl. The mixture is poured over the salad and toss to coat. Now serve immediately to dig in. Enjoy!

Arugula, Fennel, and Orange Salad

Ingredients:

½ tsp. Ground black pepper
¼ cup Olive oil
1 bunch Arugula
1 tbsp. Honey
1 tbsp. Lemon juice

½ tsp. Salt
2 Peeled and segmented orange
1 bulb thinly sliced fennel bulb
2 tbsp. Sliced black olives
Method

Combine all the ingredients in a large bowl and toss well. Serve immediately. Enjoy!

Avocado Watermelon Spinach Salad

Ingredients:

2 Large peeled, pitted and diced avocados
4 cups Cubed watermelon

4 cups spinach leaves
1 cup vinaigrette Balsamic salad dressing

Method

Combine all the ingredients in a large bowl and toss well. Serve chilled. Enjoy!

Avocado, Kale and Quinoa Salad

Ingredients

2/3 cup Quinoa
1 bunch Kale cut bite-sized pieces
½ Avocado, peeled and diced
1/3 cup Red bell pepper, chopped
½ cup Cucumber, cut into small cubes
2 tbsp. Red onion, finely chopped
1 1/3 cups Water

1 tbsp. Crumbled feta cheese
For Dressing
¼ cup Olive oil2 tbsp. Lemon juice
1 ½ tbsp. Dijon mustard
¾ tsp. Sea salt
¼ tsp. Black pepper, freshly grounded

Method

Add quinoa and water in a saucepan. Bring it to boil. Reduce the flame and cook 15 to 20 minutes. Keep it aside. Steam the kale using a steamer for 45 second. Whisk all the ingredients for seasoning in a bowl. Mix kale, quinoa, avocado, and the rest items and top it with salad dressing. Enjoy!

Zucchini Salad with Special Dressing

Ingredients

6 Small zucchini, sliced thinly
½ cup Green pepper, chopped
½ cup Onion, diced
½ cup Celery, diced
1 jar Pimientos, drained and diced
2/3 cup Vinegar

3 tbsp. White wine vinegar
1/3 cup Vegetable oil
½ cup Sugar
½ tsp. Pepper
½ tsp. Salt

Method

Mix all the vegetables in a medium sized bowl and keep aside. Mix all other ingredients in a jar with tight cover. Shake the mixture vigorously and pour it over the vegetables. Toss the veggies gently. Cover and keep it in the refrigerator overnight or minimum 8 hours. Served chilled. Enjoy!

Vegetable and Bacon Salad

Ingredients

3 cups chopped broccoli
3 cups chopped cauliflower
3 cups chopped celery
6 slices bacon
1 ½ cups mayonnaise
¼ cup Parmesan cheese
1 package frozen green peas, defrosted

1 cup sweetened dried cranberries
1 cup Spanish peanuts
2 tbsp. grated onion
1 tbsp. white wine vinegar
1 tsp. salt
¼ cup white sugar

Method

Cook bacon in a large, deep skillet until they become nicely brown. Place it on the plate and crumble. In a large bowl, mix the broccoli, cauliflower, peas, cranberries and celery together. In another bowl, mix the cheese, mayonnaise, onion, sugar, vinegar and salt together. Pour the mixture over the vegetables. Throw nuts, bacon and toss it well. Serve immediately or chilled. Enjoy!

Crunchy Cucumber Salad

Ingredients

2 quarts Small cucumbers, sliced with its   peel

2 Onions, thinly sliced
1 cup Vinegar

1 ¼ cups Sugar
1 tbsp. Salt

Method

Mix onion, cucumber and salt in a bowl and allow it to soak for 3 hours. Take a saucepan and add vinegar and warm it. Add sugar to it and stir the mixture continuously till the sugar gets dissolved. Remove the cucumber from the soaked mixture and drain extra liquid. Add cucumber into the vinegar mixture and mix it. Put the mixture into plastic freezer bags or container. Freeze it. Defrost and serve it chilled. Enjoy!

Colorful Veggie and Cheese Salad

Ingredients

1/3 cup Red or green bell pepper, diced
1 cup Celery, diced
1 packet Frozen green peas
3 Sweet pickles, finely chopped
6 Lettuce

2/3 cup Mayonnaise¾ cup Cheddar cheese, cut into cubes
Pepper, freshly grounded
Salt to taste

Method

Take a large bowl. Mix mayonnaise, pepper, and salt together. Add red or green bell pepper, pickles, celery, and peas to the mixture. Combine all the ingredients well. Add cheese to the mixture. Chill it for 1 hour. Place the lettuce leaves on the salad dish and pile the mixture on the leaves. Enjoy!

Creamy Cucumber Salad

Ingredients

9 cups Cucumbers, peeled and thinly sliced,
8 Green onions, finely chopped
¼ tsp. Onion salt
¼ tsp. Garlic salt
½ cup Yogurt

½ cup Low fat mayonnaise
¼ tsp. Pepper
2 drops Hot pepper sauce
¼ cup Evaporated milk
¼ cup Cider vinegar
¼ cup Sugar

Method

Take a large bowl. Place the cucumber, green onions, onion salt, garlic salt, and yogurt in a bowl and mix it well. Combine mayonnaise, pepper, pepper sauce, milk, vinegar, sugar and form a homogenous mixture. Spread the dressing over the cucumber mixture. Toss it well so that all the veggies get coated with the dressing. Refrigerate the salad for 4 hours. Serve it chilled. Enjoy!

Bacon and Broccoli Salad

Ingredients

1 head broccoli, sliced into bite size pieces
10 slices Bacon
¼ cup Red onion, finely chopped
½ cup Raisins

3 tbsp. White wine vinegar
1 cup Mayonnaise
1 cup Sunflower seeds
2 tbsp. White sugar,

Method

Take a large skillet. Cook the bacon till it gets evenly brown. Crumble and keep it aside. Place the broccoli, raisins and onion in a bowl and toss the mixture. Take a small bowl and whisk together the mayonnaise, vinegar, and sugar. Transfer it to the broccoli mixture and toss. Refrigerate for two hours. Before serving, add bacon and sunflower seed. Enjoy!

Vegetables and Corn Bread Salad

Ingredients

1 cup Corn bread, coarsely crumbled
1 can Whole kernel corn, drained
½ cup Onion, chopped
½ cup Cucumber, chopped
½ cup Broccoli, chopped
½ cup Green pepper and sweet red

pepper, chopped finely
½ cup Seeded tomato, chopped
½ cup Peppercorns
Ranch salad dressing
Salt & pepper to taste
Lettuce leaves

Method

Take a large bowl. Add the corn bread and veggies. Toss the mixture. Sprinkle salad dressing over the mixture. Add salt and pepper according to your taste. Toss it again. Cover the mixture and refrigerate it for a minimum of 4 hours. Put the salad on the lettuce leaves and serve. Enjoy!

Bean and Vegetable Salad

Ingredients

2 cans whole kernel corn, drained
1 can black beans, rinsed and drained
8 green onions, finely chopped
2 jalapeno peppers, de-seeded and finely chopped
1 green bell pepper, thinly sliced
1 avocado, peeled and diced

1 jar pimentos
3 tomatoes, sliced
1/2 cup Italian salad dressing
1/2 tsp. garlic salt
1 cup chopped cilantro
1 lime, juiced

Method

Mix the black beans and corn in a large bowl. Add green onions, bell pepper, jalapeno peppers, pimentos, avocado, and tomatoes and toss the mixture. Add cilantro, lime juice and Italian dressing over the mixture. Add garlic salt for seasoning. Toss it well. Serve it chilled. Enjoy!

Corn and Olive Salad

Ingredients

1 packet Frozen corn
3 Hard-cooked eggs
½ cup Mayonnaise
1/3 cup Pimiento-stuffed olives

2 tbsp. Chives, minced
½ tsp. Chili powder
¼ tsp. Ground cumin
1/8 tsp. Salt

Method

Combine the corn, sliced eggs and olives in a large bowl. Mix the mayonnaise and other ingredients for seasonings in a medium sized bowl. Add the mayonnaise to the corn mixture. Stir it well so that all the vegetables and corn get coated with the mayonnaise. Cover the bowl. Refrigerate it for 2 hours. Serve chilled. Enjoy!

Corn Salad

Ingredients

6 Corns, husked, washed and drained
3 large Tomatoes
1 Onion, thinly sliced
¼ cup basil, minced

2 tbsp. White vinegar
¼ cup Olive oil
Salt & pepper to taste

Method

Cook the corns in a pan of boiling water and drain them and keep aside to cool. Cut the kernels off the cob. Take a large salad mixing bowl. Mix corn, basil, onion, tomatoes, vinegar, salt and pepper, and oil. Toss it well. Served chilled. Enjoy!

Fresh Hungarian Salad

Ingredients

1 package frozen mixed vegetables, defrosted
1 cup cauliflowers
1/2 cup sliced green onions
1/2 cup sliced pimiento-stuffed olives

1/4 cup canola oil
3 tbsp. white vinegar
1/4 tsp. pepper
1 tsp. garlic salt

Method

Combine frozen vegetables, cauliflower, onion, and olives in a large bowl. Blend the oil, garlic salt, vinegar, and pepper in the blender. Pour the salad dressing over the vegetable mixture. Toss it well. Refrigerate for 2 hours before serve. Serve it in a nice bowl. Enjoy!

A perfect mixture of tomato, cucumber and onion

Ingredients

2 large cucumber, halved and de-seeded
1/3 cup red wine vinegar
1 tbsp. white sugar

1 tsp. salt
3 large chopped tomatoes
2/3 cup coarsely chopped red onion

Method

Combine all the ingredients together and refrigerate overnight. Serve chilled. Enjoy!

Classic Cucumber Salad

Ingredients

2 large cucumbers, peeled and sliced
1 large sweet onion, sliced
2 tsp. salt
¼ cup minced carrot
1/3 cup of vinegar

1 tsp. ground ginger
5 tsp. white sugar
¼ tsp. coarse black pepper

Method

11Combine all the ingredients together and let the cucumber marinate in the fridge overnight. Serve chilled. Enjoy!

Tomato Salad with Cherry Splash

Ingredients

4 cups halved cherry tomatoes
¼ cup vegetable oil
3 tbsp. cider vinegar
1 tsp. dried

1 tsp. dried basil
1 tsp. dried oregano
½ tsp. salt
1 tsp. white sugar

Method

Combine all the ingredients in a bowl and set aside so that the tomatoes soften a bit. Toss well and serve immediately. Enjoy!

Asparagus Salad

Ingredients

1 ½ pounds asparagus, trimmed and sliced into 2-inch pieces
1 tbsp. Rice vinegar
1 tsp. Red wine vinegar
1 tsp. Soy sauce

1 tsp. White sugar
1 tsp. Dijon mustard
2 tbsp. Peanut oil
1 tbsp. Sesame oil
1 tbsp. Sesame seeds

Method

Put the rice vinegar, soy sauce, red wine vinegar, sugar, and mustard in a covered jar and mix well. Add the peanut oil as well as sesame oil slowly, continuously whisking it until smooth. Keep it aside. Cook the asparagus in boiling water and drain them. Place the asparagus in a large sized bowl. Sprinkle the salad dressing over them. Sprinkle sesame seeds and toss. Serve immediately. Enjoy!

Pasta and Black Eyed Peas in Salad

Ingredients

6 ounces Cooked and drained small shell pasta
1 can Rinsed and drained black eyed peas

1 cup Sliced green onions
¾ cup Diced, peeled cucumber
¾ cup Diced tomato

¾ cup Diced green pepper
1 small jalapeno pepper, finely chopped
For Dressing:
3 tbsp. Canola oil
¼ cup Red wine vinegar

1 tsp. Dried basil
1 tsp. Hot pepper sauce
1 tsp. Chili powder
1 tsp. Sugar
½ tsp. Seasoned salt

Method

Combine pasta, peas, green onion, cucumber, tomato, green pepper and jalapeno pepper together in the bowl. Mix the dressing and season it with salt. Sprinkle the dressing over the vegetable mixture. Toss it well. Served it chilled. Enjoy!

Spinach and Beetroot Salad

Ingredients

½ pound Baby spinach, washed and dried
1 cup Walnuts, chopped coarsely
2 ½ tbsp. White sugar
1/3 can pickled beets
¼ cup Cider vinegar
½ tsp. Garlic powder

1 tsp. Chicken bouillon granules
4 ounces Goat cheese, crushed
½ tsp. Black pepper
½ tsp. Salt
¼ cup Vegetable oil

Method

Caramelize the walnuts in a sauce pan, by heating them along with some sugar on high heat. Process the beets with cider vinegar, garlic powder, bouillon granules, salt, rest of the sugar, and pepper in a food processor. Pour oil and mix it again until smooth. Combine the sugar coated walnuts and spinach and sprinkle the dressing into it. Sprinkle cheese and serve immediately. Enjoy!

Potato Salad with Balsamic Vinegar

Ingredients

10 Red potatoes, boiled and cubed
1 Onion, thinly sliced
1 can Quartered artichoke hearts
½ cup Red peppers, roasted then diced
1 can Black olives
½ cup Balsamic vinegar
1 tsp. Dried oregano
1 tsp. Dried basil

½ tsp. Mustard powder
3 tsp. Olive oil
2 tbsp. Fresh parsley

Method

Combine all the ingredients together in a bowl and toss well so that all the ingredients get coated with the vinegar. Refrigerate for 2-4 hours. Serve chilled. Enjoy!

Marinated Tomato Salad

Ingredients

3 Tomatoes
2 tbsp. Chopped onion
1 tbsp. Fresh basil
1 tbsp. Fresh parsley
½ clove Garlic

1/3 cup olive oil
1/4 cup red wine vinegar
1/4 tsp. pepper
Salt to taste

Method

Take a nice large dish and place the tomatoes on it. Take a covered jar and put the vinegar, olive oil, basil, parsley, minced garlic and pepper in it and shake it vigorously, so that all the ingredients get combined well. Season the mixture with a pinch of salt or as per your taste. Pour the mixture over the tomatoes. Cover it properly and refrigerate overnight or for a minimum of 4 hours. Served chilled. Enjoy!

Tasty Broccoli Salad

Ingredients

1 ½ pounds Fresh broccoli, cut into florets
3 cloves Garlic
2 tbsp. Lemon juice
2 tbsp. Rice vinegar
½ tsp. Dijon mustard

Red pepper flakes to taste
1/3 cup Olive oil
Salt and freshly grounded black pepper according to taste

Method

Add some water to a pan and add some salt to it. Bring it to a boil and add the florets to it. Cook for about 5 minutes and drain. In a small bowl, add garlic, vinegar, lemon juice, mustard, oil and red pepper flakes and whisk them together vigorously. Season with salt and pepper. Pour it over the broccoli and toss well. Keep it at room temperature for 10 minutes and then refrigerate for 1 hour. Serve it cold. Enjoy!

Corn Salad with Italian Dressing

Ingredients

1 can Whole-kernel corn
1 cup Fresh tomato, chopped finely
1 cup Cucumber, peeled and chopped
½ cup Chopped celery

½ cup Green or sweet red pepper
2 Green onions
½ cup Italian salad dressing

Method

Place the corn into a bowl and add vegetables to it one by one. Toss it well. Pour the bottled Italian salad dressing and toss again. Cover it and refrigerate for several hours. Serve chilled. Enjoy!

Asparagus and Bell Pepper Salad

Ingredients

1 ½ Fresh asparagus, trim off the ends and cut into small pieces
2 Yellow bell peppers, de-seeded and sliced
¼ cup Almond slices, toasted

1 Red onion
3 tbsp. Dijon mustard¼ cup Olive oil½ cup Parmesan cheese3 cloves Garlic minced
2 tsp. Lime juice2 tsp. Sugar1 tsp. hot sauce Salad seasoning mix to taste

Method

Take a baking sheet and place the asparagus and bell peppers in a single layer. Sprinkle olive oil over the vegetables. Set 400 degrees F or 200 degrees C and preheat the oven. Place the baking sheet and roast it for 8-10 minutes. Turn the veggies occasionally. Cool and transfer the veggies in a large bowl. Add cheese, onion, roasted almonds. Whisk rest of the olive oil, mustard powder, sugar, hot sauce, lime juice, and salad seasoning. Sprinkle over the veggies and toss. Serve immediately. Enjoy!

Tomato and Basil Salad

Ingredients

3 cups cooked rice
1 Cucumber, de-seeded and cubed
1 Red onion
2 Tomatoes

2 tbsp. Olive oil
2 tbsp. Cider vinegar
1 tsp. Fresh basil
¼ tsp. Pepper

½ tsp. Salt

Method

Take a large bowl and place the rice, cucumber, onion, tomatoes and toss them together. In a covered jar, combine olive oil, cider vinegar, basil together and mix vigorously. Add salt and pepper to taste. Sprinkle over the rice mixture and toss well. Refrigerate for several hours before serving. Enjoy!

Colorful Garden Salad

Ingredients

5 tbsp. Red wine vinegar
3 tbsp. Grape seed oil
1/3 cup Chopped fresh cilantro
2 limes
1 tsp. White sugar2 cloves Garlic minced
1 packet Frozen shelled green soybeans

1 can Black beans
3 cups Frozen corn kernels
1 pint Cherry tomatoes divided into quarters
4 Green onions thinly sliced
¾ tsp. Salt

Method

Whisk the vinegar, oil, lime juice, cilantro, garlic, sugar, and salt together in a covered jar or large bowl to form a homogenous mixture. Keep it aside. Cook the soybean till they become nicely tendered. Cook the corn for 1 minute. Drain soybean and corn from water and transfer to a large bowl. Add the dressing. Toss it gently. Add tomatoes, onion to the mixture and toss. Cover the mixture. Refrigerate 2 to 4 hours. Serve chilled. Enjoy!

Mushrooms Salad

Ingredients

1 pound Fresh mushrooms
1 Onion, finely sliced and separated into rings
Finely diced sweet red pepper, handful
2/3 cup Tarragon vinegar
½ cup Canola oil

1 tbsp. Sugar
1 garlic clove minced
Dash of hot pepper sauce
1 ½ tsp. Salt
2 tbsp. Water

Method

Add all the vegetables and other ingredients in a large bowl, except the red peppers, mushrooms and onion. Mix them well. Put mushrooms and onion to the mixture and toss gently till all the ingredients are evenly mixed. Cover the bowl and refrigerate overnight or 8 hours. Sprinkle red pepper over the salad before serving. Enjoy!

Quinoa, Mint and Tomato Salad

Ingredients

1 ¼ cups Quinoa1/3 cup Raisins2 Tomatoes 1 Onion finely chopped 10 Radishes ½ Cucumber, 1/2, diced 2 tbsp. Sliced almonds slightly toasted ¼ cup Fresh mint chopped

2 tbsp. Fresh parsley finely chopped 1 tsp. Ground cumin¼ cup Lime juice2 tbsp. Sesame oil2 ½ cups Water Salt to taste

Method

Take a saucepan and add water and a pinch of salt to. Bring it to boil and add in the quinoa and raisins. Cover it and cook on simmer for 12-15 minutes. Remove it from heat and allow to cool. Drain quinoa and transfer to a bowl. In a medium sized bowl, combine onion, radish, cucumber, almonds, and tomatoes together. Toss it gently. Mix in the quinoa. Season it with spices, oil and herbs. Add salt to taste. Refrigerate for 2 hours. Serve chilled. Enjoy!

Sauerkraut Salad Recipe

Ingredients

1 can Sauerkraut washed and drained well 1 cup Carrots grated 1 cup Green pepper finely chopped 1 jar Pimientos diced and drained

1 cup Celery thinly chopped 1 cup Onion thinly chopped ¾ cup Sugar ½ cup Canola oil

Method

Combine all the ingredients in a large bowl and mix well. Cover the bowl with a lid and refrigerate overnight or for 8 hours. Serve chilled. Enjoy!

Quick Cucumber Salad

Ingredients

4 tomatoes, sliced into 8 wedges 2 large cucumbers nicely peeled and make fine slices

¼ cup Chopped fresh cilantro 1 large red onion, finely sliced 1 fresh lime, juiced

Salt to taste

Method

Place the sliced cucumbers, tomatoes, red onion, and cilantro in a large bowl and toss well. Add lime juice to the mixture and toss gently so that all the vegetables get coated with lime juice. Season the mixture with salt. Serve immediately or can be served after refrigeration. Enjoy!

Tomato Slices with Creamy Dressing

Ingredients

1 cup Mayonnaise
½ cup Half-and-half cream
6 Tomatoes, sliced

1 Red onion cut thin into rings
¾ tsp. Dried basil
Few Lettuce leaves

Method

Combine mayonnaise and half-and-half cream together and whisk well. Add half the basil. Cover the mixture and refrigerate. Take a plate and line it with the lettuce leaves. Arrange the slices of tomatoes and onion rings. Drip the chilled dressing over the salad. Sprinkle then rest of the basils. Serve immediately. Enjoy!

Beet Salad Platter

Ingredients

4 bunches Fresh small beets stems stripped off
2 heads Belgian endive
2 tbsp. Olive oil
1 pound spring lettuce mix
1 tbsp. Lemon juice
2 tbsp. White wine vinegar

1 tbsp. Honey
2 tbsp. Dijon mustard
1 tsp. Dried thyme
½ cup Vegetable oil
1 cup Crumbled feta cheese
Salt and pepper to taste

Method

Lightly coat the beet with vegetable oil. Roast for approximately 45 minutes in preheated oven, at 450 degrees F or 230 degrees C. Peel the beet and cut into small cubes. Combine lemon juice, mustard, honey, vinegar, and thyme in a blender and process it. Gradually add olive oil while the blender is running. Add salt and pepper to taste. In a salad bowl, place spring lettuce, enough amount of dressing and mix it well. Arrange endive on a plate. Pile the green salad. Top it with beet cubes and feta cheese. Enjoy!

Chicken and Spinach Salad

Ingredients

5 cups Chicken cooked and cubed
2 cups Green grapes, cut into halves
1 cup Snow peas
2 cups Packed torn spinach
2 ½ cups Celery thinly sliced
7 0z. cooked Spiral pasta or elbow macaroni
1 jar Marinated artichoke hearts
½ Cucumber
3 sliced Green onions with tops

Large spinach leaves, optional
Orange slices, optional
For Dressing:
½ cup Canola oil
¼ cup Sugar
2 tbsp. White wine vinegar
1 tsp. Salt
½ tsp. Dried minced onion
1 tsp. Lemon juice
2 tbsp. Minced fresh parsley

Method

Mix the chicken, peas, spinach, grapes, celery, artichoke heart, cucumber, green onion and cooked pasta in a large bowl and toss. Cover it and refrigerate for a few hours. Mix the other remaining ingredients in a separate bowl and refrigerate in a covered container. Prepare the dressing just before serving the salad by combining all the ingredients and whisking it well. Mix the components and toss well and serve immediately. Enjoy!

German Cucumber Salad

Ingredients

2 large German cucumbers, sliced thinly
½ sliced Onions
1 tsp. Salt
½ cup Sour cream
2 tbsp. White sugar

2 tbsp. White vinegar
1 tsp. Dried dill
1 tsp. Dried parsley
1 tsp. Paprika

Method

Arrange cucumbers and the rings of onion in a dish. Season the vegetables with salt and keep aside for at least 30 minutes. Squeeze out excess juice from cucumbers after marinating. Mix sour cream, vinegar, dill, parsley, and sugar in a vinegar, dill, and parsley together in a bowl. Coat cucumber and onion slices in this dressing. Refrigerate overnight or at least for 8 hours. Just before serving, sprinkle paprika over the salad. Enjoy!

Colorful Citrus Salad with Unique Dressing

Ingredients

1 can Mandarin oranges¼ cup Fresh
parsley finely chopped
Leaf lettuce, optional
½ Grapefruit peeled and sectioned
½ small Cucumber
1 small Tomato sliced
½ small Red onion

½ tsp. Brown sugar
3 tbsp. French or Italian salad dressing
1 tsp. Lemon juice
1 pinch dried tarragon
1 tsp. Dried basil
¼ tsp. Pepper

Method

Place the oranges in a small bowl after draining its juice and keep aside. Reserve the juice. Take a small bowl and add parsley, basil, tarragon, salad dressing, lemon juice, orange juice, brown sugar, and pepper. Whisk the mixture until smooth. Place lettuce leaves on a plate. Arrange the fruits one by one. Drizzle the dressing over the fruits and serve. Enjoy!

Potato, Carrot and Beet Salad

Ingredients

2 Beets, boiled and sliced
4 Small potatoes, boiled and diced
2 Small carrots, boiled and sliced
3 Green onions, chopped

3 Small dill pickles, diced
¼ cup Vegetable oil
2 tbsp. Champagne vinegar
Salt to taste

Method

Combine all the ingredients and toss well to blend the flavors. Refrigerate for a few hours and serve chilled. Enjoy!

Spinach and Blackberry Salad

Ingredients

3 cups Baby spinach, washed and drained
from the water
1 pint Fresh blackberries

1 pint Cherry tomatoes
1 sliced Green onion
¼ cup finely chopped walnuts

6 ounces Crumbled feta cheese
½ cup Edible flowers

Bacon dressing or balsamic vinegar as per choice

Method

Mix baby spinach, blackberries, cherry tomatoes, green onions, walnuts together by tossing them together. Add cheese and toss again. This salad tastes good; with or without any salad dressing. If you want to add a dressing, use bacon dressing or plenty amount of balsamic vinegar as per your choice. Before serving, top with any edible flower you like. Enjoy!

Vegetable Salad with Swiss Cheese

Ingredients

1 cup Green onions, sliced
1 cup Celery, sliced
1 cup Green pepper
1 cup Pimiento-stuffed olives
6 cup Shredded lettuce

1/3 cup Vegetable oil
2 cup Shredded Swiss cheese
2 tbsp. Red wine vinegar
1 tbsp. Dijon mustard
Salt & pepper to taste

Method

Combine the olives, onions, celery, and green pepper in a salad bowl and toss well. Whisk together the oil, mustard, vinegar in a small bowl. Season the dressing with salt and pepper. Sprinkle the dressing over the vegetables. Refrigerate overnight or several hours. Before serving, line the plate with lettuce leaves. Mix cheese with the vegetables. Place the salad on the lettuce. Top it with shredded cheese. Serve immediately. Enjoy!

Tasty Carrot Salad

Ingredients

2 pounds Carrots, peeled and cut into thin diagonal slices
½ cup Flake of almonds
1/3 cup Dried cranberries
2 cups Arugula
2 cloves of Garlic minced

1 packet Crumbled Danish blue cheese
1 tbsp. Cider vinegar
¼ cup Extra-virgin olive oil
1 tsp. Honey
1-2 pinch Freshly grounded black pepper
Salt to taste

Method

Combine the carrots, garlic, and almonds in a bowl. Add a little olive oil and mix it well. Add salt and pepper to taste. Transfer the mixture to a baking sheet and bake in the preheated oven for 30 minutes at 400 degrees F or 200 degrees C. Take them out when the edge turns brown and allow them to cool. Transfer the carrot mix in a bowl. Add honey, vinegar, cranberries and cheese and toss well. Mix arugula and serve immediately. Enjoy!

Marinated Vegetable Salad

Ingredients

1 can tiny green peas, drained
1 can French-style green beans, drained
1 can White or shoe peg corn, drained
1 medium Onion, thinly sliced
¾ cup finely chopped celery

2 tbsp. Chopped pimientos
½ cup White wine vinegar
½ cup Vegetable oil
¾ cup Sugar
½ tsp. Pepper½ tsp. Salt

Method

Take a large bowl and combine peas, corns and beans. Add celery, onion and pimientos and toss the mixture well. Take a saucepan. Put all the remaining ingredients and cook on low flame. Stir continuously till the sugar gets dissolved. Pour the sauce over the vegetable mixture. Cover the bowl with a lid and refrigerate overnight. You can keep it for several days in the refrigerator. Serve chilled. Enjoy!

Roasted Colorful Corn Salad

Ingredients

8 Fresh corn in husks1 Red Bell pepper, diced
1 Green bell pepper, diced
1 red Onion, chopped
1 cup Chopped fresh cilantro
½ cup Olive oil

4 cloves of Garlic, crushed then minced
3 Limes
1 tsp. White sugar
Salt & pepper to taste
1 tbsp. hot sauce

Method

Take a large pot and place the corn in it. Pour in water and soak the corn for 15 minutes. Remove the silks from the husks of the corn and keep aside. Take a griller and preheat it at high temperature. Place the corn over the grill and cook for 20 minutes. Turn them occasionally. Allow to cool and discard the husks. Take a blender and pour the olive oil, lime juice, hot sauce in it and give it a whirl. Add in the cilantro, garlic, sugar, salt, and pepper. Blend to form a smooth mixture. Drizzle over the corn.

Serve immediately. Enjoy!

Creamy Cucumber

Ingredients

3 Cucumbers, peeled and thinly sliced
1 Onion, sliced
2 cups Water
¾ cup Heavy whipping cream

¼ cup Cider vinegar
Minced fresh parsley, optional
¼ cup Sugar
½ tsp. Salt

Method

Add water and salt the cucumber and onions, and allow to soak for at least 1 hour. Drain excess water. Whisk together the cream and vinegar in a bowl until smooth. Add the marinated cucumbers and onion. Mix well to coat evenly. Refrigerate for few hours. Before serving, sprinkle parsley. Enjoy!

Marinated Mushroom and Tomato Salad

Ingredients

12 ounces Cherry tomatoes, halved
1 package Fresh mushrooms
2 sliced green Onions
¼ cup Balsamic vinegar
1/3 cup Vegetable oil

1 ½ tsp. White sugar
½ tsp. Ground black pepper
½ tsp. Salt
½ cup Chopped fresh basil

Method

In a bowl, whisk the balsamic vinegar, oil, pepper, salt and sugar to form a homogenous mixture. Take another large bowl and mix the tomatoes, onions, mushrooms, and basil together. Toss well. Add the dressing and evenly coat the vegetables. Cover the bowl and refrigerate 3-5 hours. Serve chilled. Enjoy!

Bean Salad

Ingredients

1 can Kidney beans, washed and drained
1 can Garbanzo beans or chickpeas, washed and drained
1 can Green beans

1 can Wax beans, drained
¼ cup Julienne from green pepper
8 green Onions, sliced
½ cup Cider vinegar

¼ cup Canola oil   ½ tsp. Salt
¾ cup Sugar

Method

Combine the beans together in a large bowl. Add the green pepper and onions to the beans. In a covered jar whisk the cider vinegar, sugar, oil, and salt to form smooth dressing. Let the sugar completely dissolve in the dressing. Drizzle over the bean mixture and toss well. Cover the mixture and refrigerate overnight. Enjoy!

Beet Salad with Garlic

Ingredients

6 Beets, boiled, peeled and sliced   2 cloves of Garlic
3 tbsp. Olive oil   Salt to taste
2 tbsp. Red wine vinegar   Green onion slices, few for garnish

Method

Combine all the ingredients in a bowl and toss well. Serve immediately. Enjoy!

Marinated Corn

Ingredients

1 cup Frozen corn   2 tbsp. Lemon juice
2 green Onions, thinly sliced   ¾ tsp. Ground mustard
1 tbsp. Chopped green pepper   ¼ tsp. Sugar
1 Leaf lettuce, optional   1-2 pinch Freshly grounded pepper
¼ cup Mayonnaise

Method

Mix the mayonnaise with the lemon juice, mustard powder, and sugar together in a large bowl. Whip it well until smooth. Add corn, green pepper, onions, to the mayonnaise. Season the mixture with salt and pepper. Cover and chill it in the refrigerator overnight or at least 4-5 hours. Before serving, line the plate with lettuce and place the salad over it. Enjoy!

Pea Salad

Ingredients

8 slices Bacon
1 packet Frozen green peas, thawed and drained
½ cup chopped Celery

½ cup chopped Green onions
2/3 cup Sour cream
1 cup Chopped cashews
Salt and pepper to taste

Method

Put bacon in a large pan and cook it over medium or medium high flame till both the sides get browned. Drain extra oil with a paper towel and crumble the bacon. Keep it aside. Mix celery, peas, scallions and sour cream together in a medium sized bowl. Toss well with a gentle hand. Add cashews and bacon into the salad just before serving. Serve immediately. Enjoy!

Turnip Salad

Ingredients

¼ cup Sweet red pepper, chopped
4 cups Shredded peeled turnips
¼ cup Green onions
¼ cup Mayonnaise

1 tbsp. Vinegar
2 tbsp. Sugar
¼ tsp. Pepper
¼ tsp. Salt

Method

Take a bowl. Mix red pepper, onions and toss. Take another bowl for preparing the dressing. Mix mayonnaise, vinegar, sugar, salt and pepper and whisk it well. Pour the mixture over the vegetable and toss well. Take turnips in a bowl add this mixture to the turnip and mix well. Refrigerate the vegetable overnight or for several hours. More marinating will incorporate more taste. Serve chilled. Enjoy!

Apple and Avocado Salad

Ingredients

1 packet Baby greens
¼ cup Red onions, chopped
½ cup Chopped walnuts
1/3 cup Crumbled blue cheese
2 tsp. Lemon zest

1 Apple, peeled, cored and sliced
1 Avocado, peeled, pitted and diced
4 Mandarin oranges, juiced
½ Lemon, juiced
1 clove of Garlic minced

2 tbsp. Olive oil Salt to taste

Method

Mix the baby greens, walnuts, red onions, blue cheese, and lemon zest together in a bowl. Toss the mixture well. Whisk vigorously the mandarin orange juice, lemon zest, lemon juice, minced garlic, olive oil. Season the mixture with salt. Pour over the salad and mix. Add the apple and avocado to the bowl and toss just before serving the salad. Enjoy!

Corn, Bean, Onion Salad

Ingredients

1 can whole kernel corn, washed and drained
1 can tiny peas wash and drained
1 can Green beans, drained
1 jar Pimientos, drained
1 cup Finely chopped celery
1 Onion, finely chopped

1 Green pepper, finely chopped
1 cup Sugar
½ cup Cider vinegar
½ cup Canola oil
1 tsp. Salt
½ tsp. Pepper

Method

Take a large salad bowl and combine the onion, green pepper, celery together. Keep it aside. Take a sauce pan and pour the vinegar, oil, sugar, salt and pepper and bring it to a boil. Remove from heat and allow the mixture to cool. Drizzle over the vegetables and toss well to evenly coat the veggies. Refrigerate several hours or overnight. Served chilled. Enjoy!

Italian veggie Salad

Ingredients

1 can Artichoke hearts, drained and quartered
5 cups Romaine lettuce, rinsed, dried, and chopped
1 Red bell pepper, cut into strips
1 Carrot1 Red onion, thinly sliced
¼ cup Black olives
¼ cup Green olives
½ Cucumber

2 tbsp. Grated Romano cheese
1 tsp. Chopped fresh thyme
½ cup Canola oil
1/3 cup Tarragon vinegar
1 tbsp. White sugar
½ tsp. Dry mustard
2 cloves of Garlic minced

Method

Take a medium container with tight lid. Pour canola oil, vinegar, dry mustard, sugar, thyme, and garlic. Cover the container and whisk vigorously to form a smooth mixture. Transfer the mixture to a bowl and place artichoke hearts in it. Refrigerate and let it marinate overnight. Take a large bowl and combine the lettuce, carrot, red bell pepper, red onion, olive, cucumber, and cheese together. Toss gently. Add salt and pepper to season. Mix it with the artichokes. Allow to marinade for four hours. Serve chilled. Enjoy!

Seafood Pasta Salad

Ingredients

1 package tricolor pasta
3 stalks celery
1 pound imitation crabmeat
1 cup frozen green peas
1 cup mayonnaise

½ tbsp. white sugar
2 tbsp. white vinegar
3 tbsp. milk
1 tsp. salt
¼ tsp. ground black pepper

Method

Boil a large pot of salted water, add pasta and cook for 10 minutes. When pasta is boiling, add the green peas and crabmeat. In a large bowl, mix the other mentioned ingredients and keep aside for some time. Mix in the peas, crabmeat and pasta. Serve immediately. Enjoy!

Grilled Vegetable Salad

Ingredients

1 pound trimmed fresh asparagus
2 zucchini, halved lengthwise and end are trimmed
2 yellow squash
1 large sliced red onion
2 red bell peppers, halved and seeded.

½ cup extra virgin olive oil
¼ cup red wine vinegar
1 tbsp. Dijon mustard
1 clove minced garlic
Salt and ground black pepper to taste

Method

Heat and grill the vegetables for 15 minutes and then remove vegetables from grill and chop them into small pieces. Add other ingredients and toss the salad so that all the spices are well mixed. Serve immediately. Enjoy!

Delicious summer corn salad

Ingredients

6 ears husked and totally cleaned corn
3 large chopped tomatoes
1 large chopped onion
¼ cup chopped fresh basil

¼ cup olive oil
2 tbsp. white vinegar
Salt and pepper

Method

Take a large pot, put water and salt and boil it. Cook corn in that boil water then add all the ingredients listed. Toss the mixture well and refrigerate. Serve chilled. Enjoy!!

Crunchy Pea Salad with caramel

Ingredients

8 slices bacon
1 package dried frozen green peas
½ cup chopped celery
½ cup chopped green onions

2/3 cup sour cream
1 cup chopped cashews
Salt and pepper according to your taste

Method

Cook bacon in a pan over medium heat until browned. Mix the other ingredients, except for the cashews in a bowl. Finally add bacon and cashews over the mixture. Toss well and serve immediately. Enjoy!

Black Bean Magic Salad

Ingredients

1 can rinsed and drained black beans
2 dried cans of kernel corn
8 chopped green onions
2 seeded and minced jalapeno peppers
1 chopped green bell pepper
1 peeled, pitted and diced avocado.

1 jar pimentos
3 seeded and chopped tomatoes
1 cup chopped fresh cilantro
1 lime juiced
½ cup Italian salad dressing
½ tsp. garlic salt

Method

Take a large bowl and put all ingredients in it. Toss it well so that they mix well. Serve immediately. Enjoy!

Yummy Greek Salad

Ingredients

3 large ripe chopped tomatoes
2 peeled and chopped cucumbers
1 small chopped red onion
¼ cup olive oil
4 tsp. lemon juice

½ tsp. dried oregano
Salt and pepper according to taste
1 cup crumbled feta cheese
6 black Greek olives, pitted and sliced

Method

Take a medium sized bowl and mix the tomatoes, cucumber and onion very well and leave that mixture for five minutes. Sprinkle oil, lemon juice, oregano, salt, pepper, feta cheese and olives over the mixture. Toss and serve immediately. Enjoy!!

Amazing Thai Cucumber salad

Ingredients

3 large peeled cucumbers that must cut into ¼ inch slices and seeds are to be removed
1 tbsp. salt
½ cup white sugar

½ cup rice wine vinegar
2 jalapeno chopped peppers
¼ cup chopped cilantro
½ cup chopped peanuts

Method

Combine all the ingredients in a large mixing bowl and toss well. Season according to taste and serve chilled. Enjoy!

High protein tomato basil salad

Ingredients

4 large ripe sliced tomatoes
1 pound fresh mozzarella sliced cheese
1/3 cup fresh basil

3 tbsp. extra-virgin olive oil
Fine sea salt
Fresh ground black pepper

Method

On a plate alternate and overlap tomato and mozzarella slices. Finally put some sprinkle of olive oil, fine sea salt and pepper over it. Serve fresh, topped with the basil leaves. Enjoy!

Quick Cucumber Avocado salad

Ingredients

2 medium cubed cucumbers
2 cubed avocado
4 tbsp. chopped fresh cilantro
1 clove minced garlic
2 tbsp. chopped green onion

¼ tsp. salt
Black pepper
¼ large lemon
1 lime

Method

Take the cucumbers, avocado and cilantro mix them well. Finally add pepper, lemon, lime, onion and garlic. Toss it well. Serve immediately. Enjoy!

Mouth Watering Orzo and Tomato Salad with Feta Cheese

Ingredients

1 cup uncooked orzo pasta
¼ cup pitted green olives
1 cup diced feta cheese
3 tbsp. chopped fresh Presley

1 ripe chopped tomato
¼ cup virgin olive oil
¼ cup lemon juice
Salt and pepper

Method

Cook orzo according to the manufacturer's instructions. Take a bowl and mix the orzo, olives, parsley, dill and tomato very well. Finally put salt, pepper and on top add feta cheese. Serve immediately. Enjoy!

English Cucumber and Tomato Salad

Ingredients

8 Roma or plum tomatoes
1 English cucumber, peeled and cubed
1 cup Jicama, peeled and thinly chopped
1 small Yellow bell pepper
½ cup Red onion, cubed

3 tbsp. Lemon juice
3 tbsp. extra virgin olive oil
1 tbsp. Dried parsley
1-2 pinch of Pepper

Method

Combine together the tomatoes, bell pepper, cucumber, jicama, and red onion in a bowl. Toss well. Pour olive oil, lemon juice and coat the mixture. Sprinkle the parsley and toss. Season it with salt and pepper. Serve immediately or chilled. Enjoy!

Grandma's Eggplant Salad

Ingredients

1 Eggplant
4 Tomatoes, cubed
3 Eggs, hard-boiled, cubed
1 Onion, thinly chopped

½ cup French salad dressing
½ tsp. Pepper
Salt, for seasoning, optional

Method

Wash eggplant and cut it half lengthwise. Take a baking dish and grease it with olive oil. Arrange the eggplants cut side down in the greased baking dish. Bake for 30-40 minutes at 350 degrees F. Take it out and allow to cool. Peel the eggplant. Cut them into small cubes. Take a large bowl and transfer the eggplant to it. Add onion, tomatoes, eggs, dressing, pepper and salt. Toss well. Freeze at least 1 hour in the refrigerator and serve. Enjoy!

Carrot, Bacon and Broccoli Salad

Ingredients

2 heads Fresh broccoli, chopped
½ pound Bacon
1 bunch Green onions, chopped
½ cup Shredded carrots
½ cup Raisins, optional

1 cup Mayonnaise
½ cup Distilled white vinegar
1-2 pinch Pepper
Salt to taste

Method

Cook bacon in a large, deep pan over medium high flame until brown. Drain and crumble. Combine the broccoli, green onions, carrots and bacon in a large bowl. Add salt and pepper. Toss properly. Take a small container or bowl and put the mayonnaise and vinegar and whisk. Transfer the dressing to the vegetable mixture. Coat the vegetables with a gentle hand. Refrigerate at least 1 hour and serve. Enjoy!

Cucumber and Tomato Salad with Sour Cream

Ingredients

3-4 Cucumbers, peeled and cut slices

2 Lettuce leaves, for decoration, optional

5-7 Slices of tomatoes,
1 Onion, thinly sliced into rings
1 tbsp. Minced chives
½ cup Sour cream
2 tbsp. White vinegar

½ tsp. Dill seed
¼ tsp. Pepper
Pinch of sugar
1 tsp. Salt

Method

Place the cucumber slices in a bowl and sprinkle salt. Marinate for 3-4 hours in the refrigerator. Take out the cucumber and wash. Drain all the liquid and transfer in a large salad bowl. Add onion and keep aside. Take a small bowl and combine vinegar, sour cream, chives, dill seed, pepper and sugar in it. Whisk the mixture and pour it over the cucumber mixture. Toss gently. Arrange the plate nicely with lettuce and tomato. Serve immediately. Enjoy!

Tomato Flavored Tortellini Salad

Ingredients

1 pound Rainbow tortellini pasta
3 Plum tomatoes cut into halves
3 ounces Hard salami, diced
2/3 cup Sliced celery
¼ cup Sliced black olives
½ cup Red bell pepper
1 tbsp. Red onion, diced
1 tbsp. Tomato paste
1 clove of Garlic minced
3 tbsp. Red wine vinegar

3 tbsp. Balsamic vinegar
2 tsp. Dijon mustard
1 tsp. Honey
1/3 cup Olive oil
1/3 cup Vegetable oil
¾ cup Shredded provolone cheese
¼ cup Chopped fresh parsley
1 tsp. Chopped fresh rosemary
1 tbsp. Lemon juice
Pepper & salt to taste

Method

Cook pasta according to the instructions on the packet. Pour cold water and drain. Keep it aside. Using a broiler, broil the tomatoes until the skin becomes partially blackened. Now process tomato in the blender. Add the tomato paste, vinegars, garlic, honey and mustard and blend again. Gradually add olive oil and vegetable oil and blend until smooth. Add salt and pepper. Combine pasta with all the vegetables, herbs, salami, and lemon juice in a bowl. Pour the dressing and toss well. Serve. Enjoy!

Broccoli and Bacon in Mayonnaise Dressing

Ingredients

1 bunch Broccoli, cut into florets
½ small Red onion, finely chopped
1 cup Shredded mozzarella cheese
8 Bacon strips, cooked and crumbled

½ cup Mayonnaise
1 tbsp. White wine vinegar
¼ cup Sugar

Method

Put broccoli, cooked bacon, onion, and cheese in a large salad bowl. Toss with a gentle hand. Cover and set it aside. Mix mayonnaise, vinegar and sugar in a small container. Whisk continuously till the sugar melts and forms a smooth mixture. Pour the dressing over the broccoli mix and coat evenly. Serve immediately. Enjoy!

Chicken Salad with Cucumber Cream

Ingredients

2 cans Chicken chunks, drained from its juice
1 cup Seedless green grapes cut into halves

½ cup Chopped pecans or almonds
½ cup Chopped celery
1 can Mandarin oranges, drained
¾ cup Creamy cucumber salad dressing

Method

Take a large, deep salad bowl. Transfer the chicken, celery, grapes, oranges and pecans or almond as per your choice. Toss gently. Add cucumber salad dressing. Coat the chicken and vegetable mixture evenly with the creamy dressing. Serve immediately. Enjoy!

Vegetables with Horseradish Dressing

Ingredients

¾ cup Cauliflower florets
¼ cup Cucumber
¼ cup Chopped seeded tomato
2 tbsp. Sliced radishes
1 tbsp. Sliced green onions
2 tbsp. Diced celery
¼ cup Cubed American cheese

For Dressing:
2 tbsp. Mayonnaise
1-2 tbsp. Sugar
1 tbsp. Prepared horseradish
1/8 tsp. Pepper
¼ tsp. Salt

Method

Mix the cauliflower, cucumber, tomato, celery, radish, green onion, and cheese together in a large bowl. Keep it aside. Take a small bowl. Mix mayonnaise, sugar, horseradish until the sugar melt and forms a smooth mixture. Pour the dressing over the vegetables and toss well. Refrigerate for 1-2 hours. Serve chilled. Enjoy!

Sweet Pea and Pasta Salad

Ingredients

1 cup Macaroni
2 cups Frozen green peas
3 Eggs
3 green Onions, chopped
2 stalks Celery, chopped
¼ cup Ranch salad dressing

1 tsp. White sugar
2 tsp. White wine vinegar
2 Sweet pickles
1 cup Shredded cheddar cheese
¼ Freshly grounded black pepper

Method

Cook pasta in the boiling water. Add a pinch of salt in it. When done, rinse it with cold water and drain. Take a saucepan and fill it with cold water. Add eggs and bring it to a boil. Remove from flame and cover. Let the eggs stand in warm water for 10-15 minutes. Take the eggs out of warm water and allow to cool. Peel the skin and chop. Take a small bowl and combine salad dressing, vinegar, and sugar. Whisk well and season with salt and freshly grounded black pepper. Combine the pasta, eggs, vegetables and cheese. Pour dressing and toss. Serve chilled. Enjoy!

Colorful Pepper Salad

Ingredients

1 Green pepper, julienned
1 Sweet yellow pepper, julienned
1 Sweet red pepper, julienned
1 Purple pepper, julienned
1 Red onion, julienned
1/3 cup Vinegar

¼ cup Canola oil
1 tbsp. Sugar
1 tbsp. Minced fresh basil
¼ tsp. Salt
Dash of pepper

Method

Take a large bowl and combine all the peppers and toss it well. Add onion and toss again. Take another bowl and combine the remaining ingredients and whisk the mixture vigorously. Drizzle the dressing over the pepper and onion mixture. Toss nicely to coat the veggies. Cover the mixture and put it in the refrigerator overnight. Serve chilled. Enjoy!

Chicken, Sun-Dried Tomato and Pinenut Salad with Cheese

Ingredients

1 loaf of Italian bread, cubed
8 Grilled chicken strips
½ cup Pine nuts
1 cup Sun-dried tomatoes
4 green onions cut into 1/2-inch pieces
2 packages mixed salad greens

3 tbsp. extra virgin olive oil
½ tsp. Salt
½ tsp. freshly ground black pepper
1 tsp. Garlic powder
8 ounces feta cheese, crumbled
1 cup Balsamic vinaigrette

Method

Mix the Italian bread and olive oil. Season it with salt, garlic powder, and salt. Put the mixture in a single layer in the greased 9x13 inch baking dish. Place it in the preheated broiler and broil until it turns brown and toasted. Take it out and allow to cool. In a baking sheet line the pine nuts and place it in the bottom rack of the broiler oven and toast carefully. In a small bowl, take hot water and soak sun-dried tomatoes in it until soft. Slice the tomatoes. In a salad bowl, mix all the green veggies; add tomatoes, pine nuts, croutons, grilled chicken, vinaigrette and cheese. Toss well. Serve. Enjoy!

Mozzarella and Tomato Salad

Ingredients

¼ cup Red wine vinegar
1 clove Garlic minced
2/3 cup Olive oil
1 pint Cherry tomatoes halved
1 ½ cups Cubed part-skim mozzarella

cheese
¼ cup Chopped onion
3 tbsp. Minced fresh basil
Pepper to taste
½ tsp. Salt

Method

Take a small sized bowl. Add vinegar, minced garlic, salt and pepper and mix until the salt dissolves. Add the oil and whisk the mixture until smooth. In a large bowl, add tomatoes, cheese, onion, basil and mix it with a gentle hand. Add the dressing and toss well. Cover the bowl and put it in the refrigerator for 1 to 2 hours. Stir occasionally. Serve chilled. Enjoy!

Spicy Zucchini Salad

Ingredients

1 ½ tbsp. Sesame seeds
¼ cup Chicken broth
3 tbsp. Miso paste
2 tbsp. Soy sauce
1 tbsp. Rice vinegar
1 tbsp. Lime juice
½ tsp. Thai chili sauce

2 tsp. Brown sugar
½ cup Chopped green onions
¼ cup Chopped cilantro
6 Zucchini, julienned
2 sheets Nori cut into thin slices
2 tbsp. Slivered almonds

Method

Put sesame seeds in a pan and place over the medium flame. Cook for 5 minutes. Stir continuously. Toast it lightly. Combine the chicken broth, soy sauce, miso paste, rice vinegar, lime juice, brown sugar, chili sauce, green onions, and cilantro together in a bowl and whisk. In a large salad bowl, toss the zucchini and the dressing to coat evenly. Top the zucchini with toasted sesame seeds, almonds and nori. Serve immediately. Enjoy!

Tomato and Asparagus Salad

Ingredients

1 pound Fresh asparagus, cut into 1-inch pieces
4 Tomatoes, cut into wedges
3 cups Fresh mushrooms, sliced
1 Green pepper, julienned
¼ cup Vegetable oil

2 tbsp. Cider vinegar
1 clove Garlic minced
1 tsp. Dried tarragon
¼ tsp. Hot pepper sauce
¾ tsp. Salt
¼ tsp. Pepper

Method

In a pan, take a small amount of water and cook asparagus in it till becomes crisp and tender, nearly about 4-5 minutes. Drain and keep it aside. In a large salad bowl, combine the mushrooms with tomatoes, and green pepper. Combine other remaining ingredients in another bowl. Combine the vegetable mixture with the dressing. Toss well and cover and keep in the refrigerator for 2 to 3 hours. Serve. Enjoy!

Minty Cucumber, Onion and Tomato Salad

Ingredients

2 Cucumbers, halved lengthwise, de-seeded and sliced
2/3 cups coarsely chopped red onion
3 Tomatoes, de-seeded and coarsely chopped
½ cup Chopped fresh mint leaves

1/3 cup Red wine vinegar
1 tbsp. granulated no calorie sweetener
1 tsp. Salt
3 tbsp. Olive oil
A dash of pepper
Salt to taste

Method

Combine together the cucumbers, granulated sweetener, vinegar, and salt in a large bowl. Allow it to soak. It should be left at room temperature for at least 1 hour to marinate. Occasionally, stir the mixture. Put the tomatoes, onion, chopped fresh mint to it. Toss well. Add oil to the cucumber mixture. Toss to coat evenly. Add salt and pepper according to taste. Serve chilled. Enjoy!

Adas Salatas

(Turkish lentil salad)

Ingredients:

2 cups Lentils, cleaned
4 cups Water
¼ cup Olive oil
1 Onion, sliced
2-3 cloves Garlic, sliced
2 tsp. Ground cumin
1-2 Lemons, juice only
1 bunch Parsley, sliced

Salt and boost to taste
2 Tomatoes, cut into wedges (optional)
2 Eggs, hard-boiled and cut into wedges (optional)
Black olives, optional
¼ cup Feta milk items, optional , crumbled or sliced

Method

Add the beans and water to a huge pot and boil over medium-high fire. Decrease the heat, secure and prepare until ready through. Do not overcook. Drain and wash with cold water. Heat the olive oil in a sauté pan over medium heat. Add the red onion and sauté until just clear. Add the garlic cloves and cumin and sauté for another 1 or 2 minutes. Place the beans in a huge dish and add the red onion, tomatoes and eggs. Mix in the lemon juice, parsley, boost and salt. Serve fresh topped with the cheese. Enjoy!

Ajvar

Ingredients:

3 Medium eggplants, cut in half, lengthwise
6-8 Red sweet peppers
½ cup Olive oil

3 tbsp. Vinegar or clean fresh loaded orange juice
2-3 cloves Garlic, sliced
Salt and boost to taste

Method

Preheat the oven to 475 degrees F. Put the eggplant cut-side down on a carefully oiled baking sheet and cook until the styles are blackened and the eggplant is ready through, about 20 minutes. Remove to a huge dish and cover to steam for a few minutes. Place the sweet peppers on the baking sheet and cook in the oven, flipping, until the skin is blackened and the sweet peppers are soft, another 20 minutes or so. Remove to another dish and cover to steam for a few minutes. After the clean vegetables have chilled, remove the pulp of the eggplant into a huge dish or a mixer, eliminating the rest of the parts. Cut the sweet peppers and add them to the eggplant. Use a spud masher to mash the eggplant and sweet peppers together until smooth, but still a little coarse. If using a mixer, beat the combination to the desire structure instead. Stir in the remaining elements and season to taste. Enjoy!

Bakdoonsiyyeh

Ingredients:

2 bunches Italian parsley, sliced
¾ cup Tahini
¼ cup Lemon juice

Salt to taste
Water

Method

Whisk together the tahini, clean fresh loaded orange juice and salt in a mixing bowl until smooth. Add a tbsp. or two of water as required to make a dense dressing. Season to taste. Add the sliced parsley and toss. Serve immediately. Enjoy!

Causa Rellena

Ingredients:

2 pounds Yellow, Yukon gold celery
½ cup Oil

¼ cup Lime or clean fresh loaded orange juice

2-3 amarillo chili place, optional
Salt and boost to taste
2 cups Filling

2-3 Hard-boiled egg, sliced
6-8 Pitted black olives

Method:

Place the celery in a huge pot of salted water. Heat to a boil and cook the celery until they are soft and ready through. Keep aside. Put the celery through a ricer or mash with a spud masher until smooth. Mix in the oil, boost (if using), calcium mineral or clean fresh loaded orange juice and salt to taste. Line a lasagna pan dish. Distribute 50 % the celery into the bottom of the dish and smooth out. Distribute the preferred stuffing similarly over the celery. Distribute the remaining celery similarly over the stuffing. Lay an offering dish upside-down over the top of the causa dish. Using both hands, turn the dish and dish over, enabling the causa fall onto the dish. Garnish the causa decoratively with the hard-boiled egg and olives and, if you like, a spices. Cut into sections and provide. Enjoy!

Curtido

Ingredients:

½ head Cabbage
1 Carrot, peeled and grated
1 cup beans
4 cups Boiling water
3 sliced Scallions

½ cup White apple cider vinegar
½ cup Water
1 Jalapeno or serrano chili boost
½ tsp. Salt

Method

Place the vegetables and beans in a huge heat-proof dish. Add the sizzling water into the dish to cover the vegetables and beans and set aside for about 5 minutes. Drain in a colander, forcing out as much fluid as possible. Return the vegetables and beans to the dish and toss with the remaining of the elements. Let set in refrigerator for a couple hours. Serve chilled. Enjoy!

Gado Gado

Ingredients

1 cup Green Gram beans, boiled
2 Carrots, peeled and sliced
1 cup Green beans, cut into 2-inch measures, steamed

2 Potato, peeled, boiled and sliced
2 cups Romaine lettuce
1 Cucumbers, peeled, cut in rings
2-3 Tomatoes, cut into wedges

2-3 egg hard boiled, cut into wedges
10-12 Krupuk , shrimp crackers

Peanut Sauce

Method

Combine all the ingredients, except for the romaine lettuce, and mix well. Serve the salad on a bed of the romaine lettuce. Enjoy!

Hobak Namul

Ingredients

3 Hobak or zucchini crush, cut into half moons
2-3 cloves Garlic, chopped
1 tsp. Sugar

Salt
3 tbsp. Soy marinade
2 tbsp. Toasted sesame oil

Method

Bring a pot of water to a steam over medium-high fire. Add the crush, and cook for about 1 minute. Drain and wash with cold water. Drain again. Mix together all the ingredients and mix well. Serve warm with a selection of Japanese sides and a main meal. Enjoy!

Horiatiki Salata

Ingredients

3-4 Tomatoes, seeded and chopped
1 Cucumber, peeled, seeded and chopped
1 Red onion, sliced
½ cup Kalamata olives
½ cup Feta cheese, chopped or crumbled

½ cup Olive oil
¼ cup apple cider vinegar
1-2 cloves Garlic, chopped
1 tsp. Oregano
Salt and spice up to taste

Method

Toss the fresh vegetables, olives and dairy products together in a huge, non-reactive plate. In another plate, mix together the olive oil, apple cider vinegar, garlic cloves, oregano, spice up and add salt. Pour the dressing into the plate with the fresh vegetables and mix. Set aside to marinate for half an hour and serve it warm. Enjoy!

Kartoffelsalat

(German spud salad)

Ingredients

2 pounds apples
¾ cup hot meat or poultry soup
1 Onion, chopped
1/3 cup Oil
¼ cup Vinegar

2 tbsp. Brown or Dijon mustard
1 tbsp. Sugar
Salt and spice up to taste
1-2 tbsp. Chives or parsley, chopped, optional

Method

Place the apples into a huge pot and add enough water to cover them by inches or two. Place over medium-high warm and bring to a boil. Decrease heat to low, and continue to steam until the apples are prepared through and a knife pierces them easily. Strain and set aside to cool. Cut the apples into quarters. Combine all the ingredients together and mix well. Adjust the dish to taste and serve warm, at 70 degrees for the best taste. Enjoy!

Kvashenaya Kapusta Provansal

Ingredients

2 pounds Sauerkraut
1 Apple, cored and chopped
1-2 Carrot, peeled and grated

4-6 Scallions, chopped
1-2 tbsp. Sugar
½ cup Olive oil

Method

Add all the ingredients in a large bowl and mix well. Adjust seasoning as per taste and serve chilled. Enjoy!

Waldorf Chicken Salad

Ingredients:

Salt and pepper
4, 6- to 8-ounce boneless, skin free poultry breasts, no more than 1 inches wide heavy, trimmed
½ cup mayonnaise
2 tbsp. lemon juice
1 tsp. Dijon mustard
½ tsp. ground fennel seeds
2 celery rib cage, minced
1 shallot, minced

1 Granny Smith peeled, cored, cut in half, and cut into ¼-inch pieces
1/2 cup nuts, chopped
1 tbsp. sliced fresh tarragon
1 tsp. sliced fresh thyme

Method

Dissolve 2 tbsp. salt in 6 cups cold water in a pot. Immerse poultry in water. Heat the pot over warm water until 170 degree Celsius. Turn off the heat and let it stand for 15 minutes. Return the poultry to paper towel–lined plate. Refrigerate until poultry is chilled, about half an hour. While the poultry cools, mix mayonnaise, lemon juice, mustard, ground fennel, and ¼ tsp. boost together in large plate. Pat poultry dry with sponges and cut into ½-inch pieces. Return poultry to plate with mayonnaise mixture. Add oatmeal, shallot, the apple juice, nuts, tarragon, and thyme; toss to mix. Season with the boost and add salt to taste. Serve. Enjoy!

Lentil Salad with Olives, Excellent, and Feta

Ingredients:

1 cup beans, picked over and rinsed
Salt and pepper
6 cups water
2 cups low-sodium poultry broth
5 garlic cloves, lightly crushed and peeled
1 bay leaf
5 tbsp. extra-virgin olive oil

3 tbsp. white wine vinegar
½ cup coarsely sliced rough Kalamata olives
½ cup fresh great outcomes in, chopped
1 large minced shallot
¼ cup crumbled feta cheese

Method

Soak the beans in 4 cups of hot water with 1 tsp. of salt in it. Drain well. In a saucepan combine the beans, remaining water, broth, garlic, bay leaves and salt and cook until the beans soften. Drain and discard the garlic and bay leaves. In a bowl, combine with rest of the ingredients and mix well. Serve topped with some feta cheese. Enjoy!

Thai Grilled-Beef Salad

Ingredients:

1 tsp. paprika
1 tsp. capsicum spice up pepper
1 tbsp. white rice
3 tbsp. calcium mineral juice, 2 limes
2 tbsp. fish sauce
2 tbsp. water
½ tsp. sugar
1, 1 ½ pound flank meal, trimmed

Salt and white boost, coarsely ground
4 shallots, sliced thin
1 ½ cups fresh great outcomes in, torn
1 ½ cups fresh cilantro leaves
1 Thai Chile, stemmed and sliced thin into rounds
1 seedless English cucumber, sliced 1/4 inches wide heavy on bias

Method

Grill the flank meals on high heat until medium rare. Keep aside to rest. Slice into bite sized pieces. In a bowl combine all the ingredients and toss well until mixed. Serve immediately. Enjoy!

All-American Salad

Ingredients

1 little head red cabbage, shredded
1 large carrot, grated
1 apple, cored and chopped
Juice from, at least 50 % a Key lime
25 white seedless grapes, sliced

1/2 cup nuts, chopped
3/4 cup raisins, golden raisins look best, but I prefer regular for taste
1/2 white onion, chopped
4 tbsp. mayonnaise

Method

In the order listed, add all the elements to a large plate. Stir well after adding lime juice to all the contents. Enjoy!

"Ono-lishious": Cooked Sesame Chicken Satay Pawpaw Salad with Hoisin Balsamic Vinaigrette

Ingredients:

Chicken Satay, Skewered Chicken :
4 to 6 large poultry, cut into 1-inch cubes
1/4 cup olive oil
8 oz. hoisin spices, found in international section in grocery store
4 to 5 cloves sliced garlic
1 tsp. black pepper

1/2 tsp. white pepper
1 tsp. salt
2 tbsp. preparing sherry
12 to 16 skewers, if wooden, dip in water for 15 to 20 minutes
1/2 cup food preparation black and white sesame seeds

Method

For the Chicken Satay: Combine the first 8 elements to coat poultry. Let marinate for 2 hours. Spread poultry with the sesame plant seeds. Set aside before the food preparation.
For the Pawpaw Salad: Cut pawpaw in half, seed and skin. Cut pawpaw into quarters, and then cut into thin slices. Squeeze the calcium mineral juice over the pawpaw and arrange on plate over mixed veggies.
For the "Hoisin" Balsamic Vinaigrette: Combine the first set of elements in blender. With blender on, emulsify by such as oil slowly until well blended. Add sodium, sugar

and boost, to taste. Set aside.

Preheat BBQ grill to 400 degrees F. Place skewers on hot BBQ grill and cook for 3 minutes and then turn. Season the poultry with spices. Cook poultry for another 3 moments. Check poultry for the doneness. Place the skewers over the healthier healthy salad and take with chopped tomatoes. Drop with vinaigrette before offering. Enjoy!

Chicken Satay Healthier Healthy Salad Sammies

Ingredients

1 ½ bodyweight thin cut poultry various foods, cutlets
2 tbsp. vegetable oil
Grill planning, recommended: BBQ grill Mates Montreal Meal Seasoning by McCormick or rough sodium and pepper
3 rounded tbsp. large peanut butter
3 tbsp. black soy spices

1/4 cup any fruits juice
2 tsp. hot spices
1 lemon
1/4 seedless cucumber, cut into sticks
1 cup carrots cut into small pieces
2 cups lettuce leaves cut
4 crusty rolls, keisers or speakers, split

Method

Heat a BBQ grill pan or large non-stick package. Cover poultry in oil and BBQ grill planning and cook 3 minutes on each side in 2 batches.

Place peanut butter in a microwave safe dish and soften in the microwave on high for about 20 seconds. Mix soy, fruit juice, hot spices and lemon juice into the peanut butter. Throw poultry with satay spices. Mix the cut fresh vegetables. Place 1/4 of the fresh vegetables on sandwich bread and top with 1/4 Satay poultry mixture. Set the bun tops set up and offer or wrap for travel. Enjoy!

Cleopatra's Chicken Salad

Ingredients

1 ½ chicken breasts
2 tbsp. extra-virgin olive oil
1/4 tsp. crushed red boost flakes
4 crushed garlic cloves

1/2 cup dry white wine
1/2 orange, juiced
A handful of sliced flat leaf parsley
Coarse sodium and black pepper

Method

Heat a large non-stick package over the stove. Add extra-virgin olive oil and heat. Add the crushed boost, crushed garlic cloves and chicken breasts. Sauté the chicken breasts until carefully browned on all sides, for about 5 to 6 minutes. Let the liquid cook out and tenders cook through, about 3 to 4 minutes more, and then remove the pan from heat. Press fresh squeezed lime juice over poultry and serve with parsley boost and salt as per taste. Serve immediately. Enjoy!

Thai-Vietnamese Healthier healthy salad Bar Supreme

Ingredients

3 Latin lettuce, chopped
2 cups fresh vegetable seedlings, any variety
1 cup very perfectly sliced daikon or red radishes
2 cups peas
8 scallions, sliced on the bias
½ seedless cucumber, sliced in 1/2 lengthwise
1 pint yellow or red grape tomatoes
1 red onion, quartered and very perfectly sliced
1 selection of fresh excellent outcomes in, trimmed

1 selection fresh basil outcomes in, trimmed
2, 2-ounce packages sliced nut items, found on baking aisle
8 items almond toasted bread or anisette toasted bread, cut into 1-inch pieces
1/4 cup tamari black soy sauce
2 tbsp. vegetable oil
4 to 8 thin cut poultry cutlets, depending on size
Salt and fresh floor black pepper
1 lb. mahi mahi
1 ripe lime

Method

Combine all the ingredients in a large mixing bowl and serve chilled. Enjoy!

Christmas Cobb Salad

Ingredients

Nonstick food preparation spray
2 tbsp. walnut syrup
2 tbsp. brownish sugar
2 tbsp. apple cider
1 lb. ham meal, fully ready, large dice
½ lb. bow tie grain, cooked
3 tbsp. sliced lovely gherkins
Bibb lettuce
½ cup sliced red onion
1 cup little diced Gouda
3 tbsp. sliced fresh parsley leaves

Vinaigrette, formula follows
Marinated Organic Beans:
1 lb. peas, decrease, cut in thirds
1 tsp. sliced garlic
1 tsp. red boost flakes
2 tsp. extra-virgin olive oil
1 tsp. white vinegar
Pinch salt
Black pepper

Method

Preheat the stove to 350 degrees F. Apply non-stick cooking spray to a baking dish. In a medium-sized dish, stir together the walnut syrup, brownish glucose, and the apple cider. Add the ham and mix well. Put the ham mixture on the baking dish and bake until warmed through and the ham develops color, about 20 to 25 minutes. Remove from the oven and set aside.

Add the grain, gherkins and parsley to the dish with the vinaigrette and stir to cover. Line a large offering dish with Bibb lettuce and add the grain. Organize the red onion, Gouda, marinated peas, and ready ham in rows on top of the grain. Serve. Enjoy!

Green Potato Salad

Ingredients

7 to 8 scallions, cleaned, dried and cut into items, green and white-colored parts
1 little selection chives, sliced
1 tsp. Kosher salt
Freshly ground white pepper
2 tbsp. water
8 tbsp. extra-virgin olive oil
2 bodyweight red bliss celery, washed

3 bay leaves
6 tbsp. black vinegar
2 shallots, peeled, quartered lengthwise, sliced thin
2 tbsp. smooth Dijon mustard
1 tbsp. sliced capers
1 tsp. caper liquid
1 small bunch tarragon, chopped

Method

In a blender, blend together the scallions and chives. Season with salt as per taste. Add water and blend. Pour 5 tbsp. of the extra virgin olive oil through the top of the mixer in a slowly and blend until smooth. Bring the celery to a boil in a pot of water and reduce heat and simmer. Season the water with a touch of salt and add bay leaves in. Simmer the celery until they are tender when pierced with the tip of a blade, about 20 minutes.

In a dish large enough to hold the celery, stir together the black vinegar, shallots, mustard, capers and tarragon. Mix in the remaining extra virgin olive oil. Drain the celery and discard the bay leaves.

Place the celery in the dish and carefully grind them with the tines of a fork. Season carefully with boost and sodium and toss them well. Finish by adding the scallion and extra virgin olive oil mixture. Mix well. Keep heated at 70 degrees until serving. Enjoy!

Burnt corn salad

Ingredients

3 sweet corn cobs
1/2 a cup of sliced onions
1/2 a cup of sliced capsicum
1/2 a cup of sliced tomatoes
Salt, to taste

For the salad dressing
2 tbsp. Olive oil
2 tbsp. Lemon juice
2 tsp. Chili powder

Method

The corn cobs are to be roasted over a medium heat until they are lightly burnt. After roasting them, the kernels of the corn cobs are to be removed with a help of a knife. Now take a bowl and mix the kernels, chopped onions, capsicum and tomatoes with salt and then keep the bowl aside. Now prepare the dressing of the salad by mixing the olive oil, lemon juice and chili powder and then chill it. Before serving, pour the dressing over the salad and then serve. Enjoy!

Cabbage and grape salad

Ingredients

2 Cabbages, shredded
2 cups halved green grapes
1/2 cup finely chopped coriander
2 Green chilies, chopped

Olive oil
2 tbsp. Lemon juice
2 tsp. Icing Sugar
Salt and pepper, to taste

Method

To prepare the salad dressing take the olive oil, lemon juice with the sugar and salt and pepper in a bowl and mix them, well and then refrigerate it. Now, take the rest of the ingredients in another bowl, mix well and keep it aside. Before serving the salad, add the chilled salad dressing and mix them gently. Enjoy!

Citrus salad

Ingredients

1 cup whole wheat pasta, cooked
1/2 a cup of sliced capsicum
1/2 cup carrots, blanched and chopped
1 green onion, shredded

1/2 cup oranges, cut in segments
1/2 cup sweet lime segments
1 cup bean sprouts
1 cup curd, low-fat

2-3 tbsp. of mint leaves
1 tsp. Mustard powder

2 tbsp. Powdered sugar
Salt, to taste

Method

To prepare the dressing, add the curd, mint leaves, mustard powder, sugar and salt in a bowl and mix them well until the sugar dissolves. Mix the rest of the ingredients in another bowl and then keep it aside to rest. Before serving add the dressing to the salad and serve chilled. Enjoy!

Fruit and lettuce salad

Ingredients

2-3 Lettuce leaves, torn in pieces
1 Papaya, chopped
½ cup Grapes
2 Oranges
½ cup Strawberries

1 Watermelon
2 tbsp. Lemon juice
1 tbsp. Honey
1 tsp. Red chili flakes

Method

Take the lemon juice, honey and chili flakes in a bowl and mix them well and then keep aside. Now take the rest of the ingredients in another bowl and mix them well. Before serving, add the dressing to the salad and serve immediately. Enjoy!

Apple and lettuce salad

Ingredients

1/2 a cup of muskmelon puree
1 tsp. Cumin seeds, roasted
1 tsp. Coriander
Salt and pepper to taste
2-3 Lettuce, torn in pieces
1 Cabbage, shredded

1 Carrot, grated
1 Capsicum, cut in cubes
2 tbsp. Lemon juice
½ cup Grapes, chopped
2 Apples, chopped
2 Green onions, chopped

Method

Take the cabbages, lettuce, grated carrots and capsicum to a pot and cover them with cold water and bring them to boil and cook them until they are cooked crisp, this can take up to 30 minutes. Now drain them and tie them in a cloth and refrigerate them. Now the apples are to be taken with the lemon juice in a bowl and refrigerate it. Now take the rest of the ingredients in a bowl and mix them properly. Serve the salad immediately. Enjoy!

Bean and capsicum salad

Ingredients

1 cup Kidney beans, boiled
1 cup Chick peas, soaked and boiled
Olive oil
2 Onions, chopped
1 tsp. Coriander, chopped

1 Capsicum
2 tbsp. Lemon juice
1 tsp. Chili powder
Salt

Method

The capsicum is to be pierced with fork and then brush oil in them and then roast them over low heat. Now dip the capsicum in cold water and then the burnt skin is to be removed and then cut them in slices. Combine the rest of the ingredients with the capsicum and then mix them well. Before serving it, cool it for an hour or more. Enjoy!!

Carrot and dates salad

Ingredients

1 ½ cup of carrot, grated
1 head of lettuce

2 tbsp. of almonds, roasted and chopped
Honey and lemon dressing

Method

Take the grated carrots in a pot of cold water and keep it for about 10 minutes, then drain it. Now the same is to be repeated with the head of lettuce. Now take the carrots and lettuce with other ingredients in a bowl and refrigerate it before serving. Serve the salad by sprinkling the roasted and chopped almonds over it. Enjoy!!

Creamy pepper dressing for salad

Ingredients

2 cups of mayonnaise
1/2 a cup of milk
Water
2 tbsp. Cider vinegar
2 tbsp. Lemon juice

2 tbsp. Parmesan cheese
Salt
A dash of hot pepper sauce
A dash of Worcestershire sauce

Method

Take a large sized bowl, and take all the ingredients together in it and mix them well, so that no lump is found. When the mixture gets its desired creamy texture, pour it in your fresh fruit and veggie salad and then the salad with the salad dressing is ready to be served. This creamy and tangy dressing of pepper is not only well served with salads but can also be served with chicken, burgers and sandwiches. Enjoy!

Russian dressing

Ingredients

About 2 cups of mayonnaise
About a cup of ketchup
1/2 a cup of sweet relish

1 pinch Garlic powder
Salt and black pepper, to taste

Method

Take a large sized bowl and take all the ingredients in it and blend or whisk them well, so that the desired consistency of the salad dressing is made. When the ingredients are thoroughly mixed, keep the bowl in the refrigerator and chill the dressing. When chilled, serve with the salad that you have prepared with fresh veggies and fruits. This dressing can also be enjoyed with grilled chicken and burgers. Enjoy!

Hawaiian Salad

Ingredients

For orange dressing
A tbsp. of cornflour
About a cup of orange squash
1/2 a cup of orange juice
Cinnamon powder
For the salad
5-6 Lettuce leaves

1 Pineapple, cut in cubes
2 Bananas, cut in chunks
1 Cucumber, cut in cubes
2 Tomatoes
2 Oranges, cut in segments
4 Black dates
Salt, to taste

Method

For preparing the salad dressing, take a bowl and mix the cornflour in the orange juice and then add the orange squash to the bowl and cook it until the texture of the dressing thickens. Then the cinnamon powder and the chili powder are to be added to the bowl and then refrigerate it for few hours. Then prepare the salad, take the leaves of lettuce in a bowl and cover it with water for about 15 minutes. Now the sliced tomatoes are to be taken to a bowl with the pineapple chunks, apple, banana, cucumber and the segments of oranges in it with salt to taste and mix them well. Now add it to the lettuce leaves and then pour the chilled dressing over the salad, before serving. Enjoy!!

Burnt corn salad

Ingredients

A pack of sweet corn cob
1/2 a cup of sliced onions
1/2 a cup of sliced capsicum
1/2 a cup of sliced tomatoes
Salt, to taste

For the salad dressing
Olive oil
Lemon juice
Chili powder

Method

The corn cobs are to be roasted over a medium heat until they are lightly burnt, after roasting them, the kernels of the corn cobs are to be removed with a help of a knife. Now take a bowl and mix the kernels, chopped onions, capsicum and tomatoes with salt and then keep the bowl aside. Now prepare the dressing of the salad by mixing the olive oil, lemon juice and chili powder and then chill it. Before serving, pour the dressing over the salad and then serve. Enjoy!

Cabbage and grape salad

Ingredients

1 Cabbage head, shredded
About 2 cups of halved green grapes
1/2 a cup of finely chopped coriander
3 Green chilies, chopped

Olive oil
Lemon juice, to taste
Icing Sugar, to taste
Salt and pepper, to taste

Method

To prepare the salad dressing take the olive oil, lemon juice with the sugar and salt and pepper in a bowl and mix them, well and then refrigerate it. Now take the rest of the ingredients in another bowl and keep it aside. Before serving the salad, add the chilled salad dressing and mix them gently. Enjoy!!

Citrus salad

Ingredients

About a cup of whole wheat pasta, cooked
1/2 a cup of sliced capsicum
1/2 a cup of carrots, blanched and chopped
Spring onion. Shredded
1/2 a cup of oranges, cut in segments
1/2 a cup of sweet lime segments

A cup of bean sprouts
About a cup of curd, low-fat
2-3 tbsp. of mint leaves
Mustard powder, to taste
Powdered sugar, to taste
Salt

Method

To prepare the dressing, add the curd, mint leaves, mustard powder, sugar and salt in a bowl and mix them well. Now mix the rest of the ingredients in another bowl and then keep it aside to rest. Before serving add the dressing to the salad and serve chill. Enjoy!!

Fruit and lettuce salad

Ingredients

4 Lettuce leaves, torn in pieces
1 Papaya, chopped
1 cup Grapes
2 Oranges
1 cup Strawberries

1 Watermelon
½ cup Lemon juice
1 tsp. Honey
1 tsp. Red chili flakes

Method

Take the lemon juice, honey and chili flakes in a bowl and mix them well and then keep aside. Now take the rest of the ingredients in another bowl and mix them well. Before serving, add the dressing to the salad. Enjoy!

Curry chicken salad

Ingredients

2 Skinless, boneless chicken breasts, cooked and cut into halves
3 - 4 Stalks of celery, chopped
1/2 a cup of mayonnaise, low in fat

2-3 tsp. of curry powder

Method

Take the cooked boneless, skinless chicken breasts with, the rest of the ingredients, celery, low fat mayonnaise, curry powder in a medium sized bowls and mix them properly. Thus this delicious and easy recipe is ready to be served. This salad can be used as stuffing of sandwich with lettuce over the bread. Enjoy!!

Strawberry spinach salad

Ingredients

2 tsp. Sesame seeds
2 tsp. Poppy seeds
2 tsp. White sugar
Olive oil
2 tsp. Paprika
2 tsp. White vinegar
2 tsp. Worcestershire sauce

Onion, minced
Spinach, rinsed and torn in pieces
A quart of strawberries, chopped into pieces
Less than a cup of almonds, silvered and blanched

Method

Take a medium sized bowl; mix the poppy seeds, sesame seeds, sugar, olive oil, vinegar and paprika together with the Worcestershire sauce and onion. Mix them properly and cover it and then freeze it at least for an hour. Take another bowl and mix the spinach, strawberries and almonds together and then pour the herb mixture to it and then refrigerate the salad before serving for at least for 15 minutes. Enjoy!

Sweet restaurant slaw

Ingredients

A 16 ounce bag of coleslaw mix
1 Onion, diced
Less than a cup of creamy salad dressing
Vegetable oil

1/2 a cup of white sugar
Salt
Poppy seeds
White vinegar

Method

Take a large sized bowl; mix the coleslaw mix and the onions together. Now take another bowl and mix together the salad dressing, vegetable oil, vinegar, sugar, salt and poppy seeds together. After mixing them well, add the mixture to the coleslaw mix and coat well. Before serving the delicious salad, refrigerate it for at least an hour or two. Enjoy!

Classic macaroni salad

Ingredients

4 cups of elbow macaroni, uncooked
1 cup of mayonnaise
Less than a cup of distilled white vinegar
1 cup of white sugar
1 tsp. Yellow mustard
Salt

Black pepper, ground
A large sized onion, finely chopped
About a cup of carrots, grated
2-3 stalks of celery
2 Pimento peppers, chopped

Method

Take a large sized pot and take salted water in it and bring to boil, add the macaroni to it and cook them and let them cool for about 10 minutes and then drain it. Now take a large sized bowl and add the vinegar, mayonnaise, sugar, vinegar, mustards, salt and pepper and mix them well. When mixed well, add the celery, green peppers, pimento peppers, carrots and macaroni and again mix them well. After all the ingredients are mixed well, let it refrigerate for at least 4-5 hours before serving the delicious salad. Enjoy!

Roquefort pear salad

Ingredients

Lettuce, torn on pieces
About 3-4 pears, peeled and chopped
A can of Roquefort cheese, shredded or crumbled
Green onions, sliced
About a cup of white sugar

1/2 a can of pecans
Olive oil
2 tsp. Red wine vinegar
Mustard, to taste
A clove of garlic
Salt and black pepper, to taste

Method

Take a pan and heat oil over a medium heat, then stir the sugar with the pecans in it and keep them stirring until the sugar is melted and the pecans get caramelized, and then let them cool. Now take another bowl and add the oil, vinegar, sugar, mustard, garlic, salt and black pepper and blend them well. Now mix the lettuce, pears, and blue cheese, avocado and green onions in a bowl and then add the dressing mixture to it and then sprinkle the caramelized pecans and serve. Enjoy!!

Barbie's tuna salad

Ingredients

A can of white tuna
½ cup Mayonnaise
A tbsp. of parmesan style cheese
Sweet pickle, to taste
Onion flakes, to taste

Curry powder, to taste
Dried parsley, to taste
Dill weeds, dried, to taste
Garlic powder, to taste

Method

Take a bowl and add all the ingredients to it and mix well. Before serving, let them cool for an hour. Enjoy!!

Holiday chicken salad

Ingredients

1 pound Chicken meat, cooked
A cup of mayonnaise
A tsp. of paprika
About two cups of cranberries, dried

2 Green onions, finely chopped
2 Green bell peppers, minced
A cup of pecans, chopped
Salt and black pepper, to taste

Method

Take a medium sized bowl, mix the mayonnaise, paprika and then season them to taste and add salt if needed. Now take the cranberries, celery, bell peppers, onions and nuts and mix them well. Now the cooked chicken is to be added and then mix them again well. Season them to taste and then if required add the ground black pepper to it. Before serving, let it cool for at least an hour. Enjoy!!

Mexican bean salad

Ingredients

A can of black beans
A can of kidney beans
A can of cannellini beans
2 Green bell peppers, chopped
2 Red bell peppers
A pack of frozen corn kernels
1 Red onion, finely chopped

Olive oil
1 tbsp. Red wine vinegar
½ cup Lemon juice
Salt
1 Garlic, mashed
1 tbsp. Cilantro
1 tsp. Cumin, ground

Black pepper   1 tsp. Chili powder
1 tsp. Pepper sauce

Method

Take a bowl and mix the beans, bell peppers, frozen corn and red onions together. Now take another small sized bowl, mix the oil, red wine vinegar, lemon juice, cilantro, cumin, black pepper and then season to taste and add the hot sauce with the chili powder to it. Pour the dressing mix to it and mix well. Before serving, let them cool for about an hour or two. Enjoy!!

Bacon ranch pasta salad

Ingredients

A can of uncooked tricolor rotini pasta   1 tsp. Garlic pepper
9-10 slices of bacon   1/2 a cup of milk
A cup of mayonnaise   1 Tomato, chopped
Salad dressing mix   A can of black olives
1 tsp. Garlic powder   A cup of cheddar cheese, shredded

Method

Take salted water in a pot and bring to boil. Cook the pasta in it until softens for about 8 minutes. Now take a pan and heat the oil in a pan and cook the bacons in it and when cook drain it and then chop it. Take another bowl and add the remaining ingredients to it and then add it with the pasta and bacons. Serve when mixed properly. Enjoy!!

Red skinned potato salad

Ingredients

4 New red potatoes, cleaned and scrubbed   A stalk of celery, chopped
2 Eggs   About 2 cups of mayonnaise
A pound of bacon   Salt and pepper, to taste
Onion, finely chopped

Method

Take salted water to a pot and bring it to boil and then add the new potatoes to the pot and cook them for about 15 minutes, until tendered. Then drain the potatoes and let them cool. Now take the eggs to a pan and cover it with cold water and then bring the water to boil and then remove the pan from the heat and then keep it aside. Now cook the bacons and drain it and set it at a side. Now add and the ingredients with the potatoes and bacon and mix well. Chill it, and serve. Enjoy!!

Black bean and couscous salad

Ingredients

A cup of couscous, uncooked
About two cups of chicken broth
Olive oil
2-3 tbsp. Lime juice
2-3 tbsp. Red wine vinegar
Cumin

2 Green onions, chopped
1 Red bell pepper, chopped
Cilantro, freshly chopped
A cup of frozen corn kernels
Two cans of black beans
Salt and pepper, to taste

Method

Boil the chicken broth and then stir the couscous, and cook it by covering the pan and then leave aside. Now mix the olive oil, lime juice, vinegar and cumin and then add the onions, pepper, cilantro, corn, beans and coat it. Now mix all ingredients together, and then before serving let it cool for few hours. Enjoy!!

Greek chicken salad

Ingredients

2 cups of chicken meat, cooked
1/2 a cup of carrots, sliced
1/2 a cup of cucumber
About a cup of black olives, chopped

About a cup of feta cheese, shredded or crumbled
Italian-style salad dressing

Method

Take a large sized bowl, take the cooked chicken, carrots, cucumber, olives and cheese and mix them well. Now add the salad dressing mix to it and again mix them well. Now refrigerate the bowl, by covering it. Serve when chill. Enjoy!!

Fancy chicken salad

Ingredients

½ cup Mayonnaise
2 tbsp. Cider vinegar
1 Garlic, minced

1 tsp. Fresh dill, finely chopped
A pound of cooked skinless and boneless chicken breasts

½ cup Feta cheese, shredded   1 Red bell pepper

Method

The mayonnaise, vinegar, garlic and dill are to be blended well and are to be refrigerated for at least 6-7 hours or overnight. Now the chicken, peppers, and cheese are to be stirred with it and then let it cool for few hours and then serve the healthy and delicious recipe of salad. Enjoy!!

Fruity curry chicken salad

Ingredients

4-5 chicken breasts, cooked
A stalk of celery, chopped
Green onions
About a cup of golden raisins
Apple, peeled and sliced

Pecans, toasted
Green grapes, deseeded and halved
Curry powder
A cup of low fat mayonnaise

Method

Take a large sized bowl and take all the ingredients, like that of the celery, onions, raisins, sliced apples, toasted pecans, seedless green grapes with curry powder and mayonnaise to it and mix them well. When they are combined well with each other, let them rest for a few minutes and then serve the delicious and healthy chicken salad. Enjoy!!

Wonderful chicken curry salad

Ingredients

About 4-5 skinless and boneless chicken breasts, cut in halves
A cup of mayonnaise
About a cup of chutney
A tsp. of curry powder

About a tsp. of pepper
Pecans, about a cup, chopped
A cup of grapes, deseeded and halved
1/2 a cup of onions, finely chopped

Method

Take a large sized pan, cook the chicken breasts in it for about 10 minutes and when cooked, tear it in to pieces with the help of a fork. Then drain them and let it cool. Now take another bowl, and add the mayonnaise, chutney, curry powder, and pepper and mix then together. Then stir the cooked and torn chicken breasts in the mix and then pour the pecans, curry powder and pepper in it. Before serving, refrigerate the salad for few hours. This salad is an ideal choice for burgers and sandwiches. Enjoy!

Spicy carrot salad

Ingredients

2 Carrots, chopped
1 Garlic, minced
About a cup of water2-3 tbsp. Lemon juice
Olive oil

Salt, to taste
Pepper, to taste
Red pepper flakes
Parsley, fresh and chopped

Method

Take the carrots to the microwave and cook it for few minutes with the minced garlic and water. Take it out from the microwave, when the carrot is cooked and is softened. Then drain the carrots and set it aside. Now the lemon juice, olive oil, pepper flakes, salt and parsley are to be added to the bowl of carrots and mix them well. Let it cool for few hours and then the spicy delicious salad is ready to be served. Enjoy!!

Asian apple slaw

Ingredients

2-3 tsp. Rice vinegar 2-3 tbsp. Lime juice
Salt, to taste
Sugar
1 tsp. Fish sauce

1 Julienned jicama
1 Apple, chopped
2 Scallions, finely chopped
Mint

Method

The rice vinegar, salt, sugar, lime juice and the fish sauce are to be mixed properly in a medium sized bowl. When they are mixed properly, the julienned jicamas are to be tossed with the chopped apples in the bowl and mix them well. Then the scallion chops and the mint are to be added and mixed. Before serving the salad with your sandwich or burger, let it cool for a while. Enjoy!!

Squash and orzo salad

Ingredients

1 Zucchini
2 Scallions, chopped
1 Yellow squash

Olive oil
A can of cooked orzo
Dill

Parsley
½ cup Goat cheese, shredded

Pepper and salt, to taste

Method

The zucchini, chopped scallions with the yellow squash are to be sautéed in olive oil over medium heat. These are to be cooked for few minutes until they are softened. Now transfer them to a bowl and tip the cooked orzo in the bowl, with parsley, shredded goat cheese, dill, salt and pepper and then mix it again. Before serving the dish, cool the salad for few hours. Enjoy!!

Salad with Watercress-fruit

Ingredients

1 Watermelon, cut into cubes
2 Peaches, cut into wedges
1 bunch Watercress
Olive oil

½ cup Lemon juice
Salt, to taste
Pepper, to taste

Method

The cubes of watermelon and the wedges of peaches are to be tossed together with the watercress in a medium sized bowl and then sprinkle the olive oil over it with the lime juice. Then season them to taste and if required add the salt and pepper, according to taste. When all the ingredients are easily and properly mixed, keep it aside or it can also be kept in the refrigerator for few hours and then the delicious to taste, yet healthy fruit salad is ready to be served. Enjoy!!

Caesar Salad

Ingredients

3 Cloves of garlic, minced
3 Anchovies
½ cup Lemon juice
1 tsp. Worcestershire sauce
Olive oil

An egg yolk
1 head Romaine
½ cup Parmesan style cheese, shredded
Croutons

Method

The minced cloves of garlic with anchovies and lemon juice are to be pureed, then the Worcestershire sauce are to be added to it with the salt, pepper and yolk and then blend it again, until smooth. This blend is to be done with the help of a blender on a slow setting, now the olive oil is to be added slowly and gradually with it and then the romaine is to be tossed in it. Then the mixture is to be set aside for a while. Serve the salad with topping of parmesan cheese and croutons. Enjoy!!

Chicken Mango Salad

Ingredients

2 Chicken breasts, boneless, cut in pieces
Mesclun greens
2 Mangoes, cut in cubes
¼ cup Lemon juice

1 tsp. Ginger, grated
2 tsp. Honey
Olive oil

Method

The lemon juice and honey is to be whisked in a bowl and then add the grated ginger to it and also add the olive oil to it. After mixing the ingredients in the bowl well, keep it aside. Then the chicken is to be grilled and then let it cool, and after cooling it tears the chicken in bite friendly cubes. Then take the chicken to the bowl and toss it well with the greens and the mangoes. After mixing all the ingredients well, keep it aside to cool then serve the delicious and interesting salad. Enjoy!!

Orange salad with mozzarella

Ingredients

2-3 oranges, cut into slices
Mozzarella
Fresh basil leaves, torn in pieces

Olive oil
Salt, to taste
Pepper, to taste

Method

The mozzarella and the slices of orange are to be mixed together, with the fresh torn leaves of basil. After mixing them well, sprinkle the olive oil over it the mixture and season to taste. Then if required add salt and pepper, to taste. Before serving the salad, let the salad cool for few hours as this will give the salad the correct flavors. Enjoy!!

Three-bean salad

Ingredients

1/2 a cup of cider vinegar

About a cup of sugar

A cup of vegetable oil
Salt, to taste
½ cup Green beans
½ cup Wax beans

½ cup Kidney beans
2 Red onions, finely chopped
Salt and pepper, to taste
Parsley leaves

Method

The cider vinegar with the vegetable oil, sugar and salt are to be taken in a pot and bring them to boil, then add the beans to it with the sliced red onions and then marinate it for at least an hour. After an hour, season to taste the salt, add salt and pepper, if required and then serve it with the fresh parsley. Enjoy!!

Miso tofu salad

Ingredients

1 tsp. Ginger, finely chopped
3-4 tbsp. of miso
Water
1 tbsp. of rice wine vinegar
1 tsp. Soy sauce

1 tsp. Chili paste
1/2 a cup of peanut oil
A baby spinach, chopped
½ cup Tofu, cut in chunks

Method

The chopped ginger is to be pureed with miso, water, rice wine vinegar, soy sauce and chili paste. Then this mixture is to be blended with half a cup of peanut oil. When they are mixed properly, add the cubed tofu and the chopped spinach to it. Chill & serve. Enjoy!!

Japanese radish Salad

Ingredients

1 Watermelon, cut in slices
1 Radish, sliced
1 Scallion
1 bunch Baby greens
Mirin
1 tsp. Rice wine vinegar

1 tsp. Soy sauce
1 tsp. Ginger, grated
Salt
Sesame oil
Vegetable oil

Method

Take the watermelon, radish with the scallions and green in a bowl and keep it aside. Now take another bowl, add the mirin, vinegar, salt, grated ginger, soy sauce with the sesame oil and the vegetable oil and then mix them well. When the ingredients in the bowl in mixed well, spread this mixture over the bowl of watermelons and radish. Thus the interesting yet very delicious salad is ready to be served. Enjoy!!

Southwestern Cobb

Ingredients

1 cup Mayonnaise
1 cup Buttermilk
1 tsp. Hot Worcestershire sauce
1 tsp. Cilantro
3 Scallions
1 tbsp. Orange zest
1 Garlic, minced

1 head Romaine
1 Avocado, diced
Jicama
½ cup Sharp cheese, shredded or crumbled
2 Oranges, cut into segments
Salt, to taste

Method

The mayonnaise and the buttermilk are to be pureed with the hot Worcestershire sauce, scallions, orange zest, cilantro, minced garlic and salt. Now take another bowl and toss the romaine, avocados and the jicamas with oranges and the shredded cheese. Now pour the puree of the buttermilk over the bowl of oranges and keep it aside, before serving, so that the correct flavor of the salad is gained. Enjoy!!

Pasta Caprese

Ingredients

1 packet Fusilli
1 cup Mozzarella, diced
2 Tomatoes, deseeded and chopped
Fresh leaves of basil

¼ cup Pine nuts, toasted
1 Garlic, minced
Salt and pepper, to taste

Method

The fusilli is to be cooked according to the instructions and then is to be kept aside to cool. After it is cooled, mix it with mozzarella, tomatoes, toasted pine nuts, minced garlic and basil leaves and season to taste, and add salt and pepper, if required, according to taste. Keep the whole mixture of the salad aside to cool and then serve it with your sandwiches or burgers or any of your meals. Enjoy!!

Smoked-Trout Salad

Ingredients

2 tbsp. Cider vinegar
Olive oil
2 Shallots, minced
1 tsp. Horseradish
1 tsp. Dijon mustard
Arugula

1 tsp. Honey
Salt and pepper, to taste
1 Can Smoked trout, flaked
2 apples, cut in slices
2 Beets, sliced

Method

Take a large sized bowl and toss in it the flaked smoked trout with julienned apples, beets and arugula and then keep the bowl aside. Now take another bowl and mix the cider vinegar, olive oil, horseradish, minced shallots, honey and Dijon mustard and then season the mixture to taste and then if required add salt and pepper, according to your taste. Now take this mixture and pour over the bowl of julienned apples and mix well and then serve the salad. Enjoy!!

Egg salad with Beans

Ingredients

1 cup Green beans, blanched
2 Radishes, sliced
2 Eggs

Olive oil
Salt and pepper, to taste

Method

The eggs are to be chard boiled at first and then mix it with the blanched green beans, sliced radishes. Mix them well, and then sprinkle over them olive oil and add salt and pepper, according to taste. When all the ingredients are mixed properly, keep it aside and let them cool. When the mix is cooled, the salad is ready to be served. Enjoy!!

Ambrosia Salad

Ingredients

1 cup Coconut milk
2-3 slices Orange zest
A few drops Vanilla essence
1 cup Grapes, sliced

2 Tangerines, sliced
2 Apples, cut into slices
1 Coconut, grated and toasted
10-12 Walnuts, smashed

Method

Take a medium sized bowl and mix the coconut milk, orange zest with vanilla essence. When whisked properly add the sliced tangerine with the sliced apples and grapes. After mixing all the ingredients properly, refrigerate it for an hour or two, before serving the delicious salad. When the salad is cooled, serve the salad with sandwich or burgers. Enjoy!!

Wedge salad

Ingredients

A cup of mayonnaise
A cup of blue cheese
1/2 a cup of buttermilk
A shallot
Lemon zest
Worcestershire sauce

Fresh leaves of parsley
Iceberg wedges
1 Egg, hard boiled
1 cup Bacon, crumbled
Salt and pepper, to taste

Method

The mayonnaise with the blue cheese, buttermilk, shallot, sauce, lemon zest and parsley are to be pureed. After making the puree, season it to taste and if required add the salt and pepper, according to taste. Now take another bowl and toss the iceberg wedges into the bowl with the egg mimosa, for making the egg mimosa stain the hard boiled eggs through the strainer. Now pour the mayo puree over the bowl of wedges and mimosa and then mix it well. The salad is to be served by spreading the fresh bacon over it. Enjoy!!

Spanish pimiento salad

Ingredients

3 Scallions
4-5 Olives
2 Pimientos
2 tbsp. Sherry vinegar
1 head Paprika, smoked

1 head Romaine
1 handful Almonds
A clove of garlic
Bread slices

Method

The scallions are to be grilled and then are to be chopped in pieces. Now take another bowl and toss the pimientos and the olives in it with the almonds, smoked paprika, vinegar, romaine and the grilled and chopped scallions. Mix the ingredients of the bowl properly and keep it aside. Now the slices of the bread are to be grilled and when grilled the cloves of garlic are to be rubbed over the slices and then pour the mixture of the pimientos over the grilled breads. Enjoy!!

Mimosa salad

Ingredients

2 Eggs, hard boiled
½ cup Butter
1 head Lettuce

Vinegar
Olive oil
Herbs, chopped

Method

Take a medium sized bowl and mix the lettuce, butter with the vinegar, olive oil and the chopped herbs. After mixing the ingredients of the bowl properly, keep the bowl aside for a while. In the meantime, the mimosa is to be prepared. For preparing the mimosa, the hard boiled eggs are to be peeled at first and then with a help of a strainer, strain the hard boiled eggs and thus the egg mimosa is ready. Now this egg mimosa is to be spooned over the bowl of salad, before serving the delicious mimosa salad. Enjoy!!

Classic Waldorf

Ingredients

1/2 a cup of mayonnaise
2-3 tbsp. Sour cream
2 Chives
2-3 tbsp. Parsley
1 Lemon zest and juice

Sugar
2 Apples, chopped
1 stalk Celery, chopped
Walnuts

Method

Take a bowl and then the mayonnaise, sour cream is to be whisked with chives, lemon zest and juice, parsley, pepper and sugar. When the ingredients in the bowl are mixed properly keep it aside. Now take another bowl, and toss the apples, chopped celery and walnuts in it. Now take the mayo mixture and toss it with the apples and celery. Mix all the ingredients well, rest the bowl for a while and then serve the salad. Enjoy!!

Black eyed pea salad

Ingredients

Lime juice
1 Garlic, minced
1 tsp. Cumin, ground
Salt
Cilantro
Olive oil

1 cup Black-eyed peas
1 Jalapeno, minced or smashed
2 Tomatoes, cut into dices
2 Red onions, finely chopped
2 Avocados

Method

The lime juice is to be whisked with the garlic, cumin, cilantro, salt and olive oil. When all these ingredients are properly mixed, toss this mixture with the smashed jalapenos, black eyed peas, avocados and the finely chopped red onions. When all the ingredients are mixed properly, give the salad a standing time for few minutes and then serve. Enjoy!!

Creamy crunchy slaw

Ingredients

A cup of mayonnaise
2 tbsp. Cider vinegar
1 tsp. Caraway seeds
1 head Cabbages, shredded

2 Scallions, chopped
2 Green apples, cut into slices
1 cup Bacon
Salt and pepper, to taste

Method

The mayonnaise is to be mixed it the caraway seeds and the cider vinegar. When mixed properly, toss the mixture with the finely chopped cabbages, scallion, green apples and cooked bacons. Now mix the ingredients well, and then season to taste, if required add salt and pepper, to taste and then keep aside for a while before serving. Enjoy!!

Bistro bacon salad

Ingredients

1 cup Bacon
2 tbsp. Cider vinegar
1 tsp. Dijon mustard

Olive oil
1 bunch mesclun greens
Salt and pepper, to taste

1 Egg, poached

Method

The bacons are to be fried at first and then the fried bacons are to be chopped. Now mix the cider vinegar, Dijon mustard, olive oil, salt and pepper in a bowl. After mixing all these ingredients properly, toss this mixture with the mesclun greens. Then top the salad with the chopped bacons and poached egg. Enjoy!!

Curried tuna salad

Ingredients

1 tsp. Curry powder
Vegetable oil
½ cup A cup of mayonnaise
Lime juice
A can of tuna

2 Red onions, cut into slices
1 bunch Cilantro
10-12 Golden raisins
Salt and pepper, to taste

Method

The curry powder is to be toasted in the vegetable oil and then keep it aside to cool. Now take the mayonnaise, lime juice, salt and pepper to a bowl and mix them well. Now take the toasted powder and this mixture and toss it with the canned tune, cilantro, red onions and raisin. Mix them well and then serve the delicious to taste, interesting salad. Enjoy!!

Cranberry spinach salad

Ingredients

½ cup Butter
Less than a cup of almonds, blanched
A pound of spinach, chopped in pieces
A cup of cranberries, dried
1 tsp. Sesame seeds, toasted
1 tsp. Poppy seeds

1/2 a cup of white sugar
1 Onion, minced
1 tsp. Paprika
About 1/2 a cup of white wine vinegar
Cider vinegar
1/2 a cup of vegetable oil

Method

Take a pan and melt the butter in it in the oil over a low heat and then mix the almonds in it and toast it. And when toasted, let it cool for a while. Now take another medium sized bowl, mix the sesame seeds, poppy seeds, sugar, onion, with the white wine vinegar, cider vinegar and the oil. Then mix this mixture with the spinach and finally toss it in the bowl of toasted almonds and the dried cranberries. Then the salad is ready to be served. Enjoy!!

Bermuda spinach salad

Ingredients

5-6 Eggs
1/2 a pound of bacon
About two pounds of spinach, finely chopped
3 Croutons
1 cup Mushrooms

1 Onion
A cup of white sugar
Vegetable oil
1 tsp. Black pepper, ground
Celery seeds
1 tsp. Dijon mustard

Method

Take the eggs to a pan and cover the pan wholly with cold water and then bring the water to boil, and then let the egg settle in the water, so keep the pan aside and cool it. When the eggs are cool, peel and chop them. Now take the bacons to a pan and cook it until brown in color. After cooking them, drain it. Now take the rest of the ingredients and mix it well. When mixed well, the salad is ready to be served. Enjoy!!

Spinach and mushroom salad

Ingredients

1 pound Bacon, cut into slices
3 Eggs
1 tsp. White sugar
2-3 tbsp. of water

2 tbsp. of cider vinegar
A pound of spinach
Salt
About a pound of mushrooms, cut in slices

Method

Take a large sized pan, and cook the slices of bacon in oil over a medium heat. When the bacons turn its color to brown, crumble it and set it aside and at the same time the bacon fat is to be reserved. Now take the eggs to the pan and cover in with water and then bring the water to boil. After sometime take the eggs out and cool, then peel and cut the eggs in wedges. Now take the sugar, water, vinegar and salt to the pan with the bacon fat and heat them thoroughly. Now take all the ingredients with the spinach to a large sized bowl, mixed them and thus the delicious salad is ready to be served. Enjoy!!

Wilted Spinach Salad

Ingredients

3 Eggs
A pound of bacon, sliced
Bunch of spinach, cleaned and dried
About a cup of sugar

1/2 a cup of white vinegar
A cup of red wine vinegar
3 Green onions

Method

Take the eggs to a pan and cover them with sufficient cold water and then bring the water to boil, by covering the pan. When the eggs are done, set in aside to cool and then peel and cut the eggs in slices or wedges. Now take the bacons to the pan and cook them over a low heat. When the bacons are browned in color, transfer them to a large sized bowl with the spinach and green onions. Pour the bacon fat and the rest of the ingredients to the bowl, mix well and then the salad is ready to be served. Enjoy!!

Warm Brussels Sprouts, Bacon and spinach salad

Ingredients

6-7 Bacon slices
2 cups of Brussels sprouts
1 tsp. Caraway seeds
2 tbsp. Vegetable oil

2 tbsp. White wine vinegar
1/2 pound of spinach, chopped, rinsed and dried

Method

The bacon is to be taken to a pan and cooked over a medium heat, until the bacon is browned in color. After it is cooked, crumble and then set them aside. Now the sprouts are to be steamed until they are softened. In the remaining bacon fat of the pan, add the sprouts with the caraway seeds and stir them for a minute or two until they are tendered. Now take all the ingredients along with the bacons, spinach to a bowl and then mix well. When mixed well, the delicious salad is ready to serve. Enjoy!!

Broccoli Salad

Ingredients

1 cup of low fat mayonnaise
2 Broccoli heads, fresh, cut in pieces
1/2 cup of red onions, finely chopped

1/2 cup of raisin
2 tbsp. White wine vinegar
1 tsp. White sugar1 cup of sunflower

seeds

Method

Take the bacons to a pan and cook them over medium heat, until they are browned. Then drain the bacons and keep it at a side. Now take all the ingredients to a bowl, along with the cooked bacon and mix them well. When they are mixed, refrigerate it for an hour or two and then serve it chilled. Enjoy!!

Harvest Salad

Ingredients

1/2 cup of walnuts, chopped
1 bunch of spinach, cleaned and torn in bites
1/2 a cup of cranberries
1/2 cup of blue cheese, shredded or crumbled

2 Tomatoes, deseeded and chopped
1 avocado, peeled and cut in dice
2 tbsp. Red wine vinegar
2 tbsp. Red raspberry jam
1 cup of walnut oil
Salt and black pepper, to taste

Method

The oven is to be preheated to 190C and then the walnuts are to be arranged in a baking sheet and are to be then toasted until they are browned. Now take a bowl and mix the spinach, walnuts, cranberries, red onions, avocado, blue cheese and tomatoes. When mixed properly, take another small sized bowl and mix the jam, walnut oil, pepper and salt and the vinegar. Now pour this mixture to the salad and mix them well. Before serving cool it for an hour or two. Enjoy!!

Winter green salad

Ingredients

1 bunch Collard leaves, chopped
1 bunch of kale leaves, chopped
1 Romaine lettuce, trimmed
1 head of red cabbage
1 pear
1 Bermuda onion
1 Avocado, peeled and diced
2 Carrots, grated
2-3 tbsp. Raisins
Olive oil

Vinegar
1 tsp. Honey
1 tsp. Oregano
1 tsp. Dijon mustard
1 Garlic clove, minced
Peppercorns

Method

Take a large sized bowl and toss the collard leaves, kale, and grated carrots with the cabbage, walnuts, tomatoes and raisins and mix them together. Now take another small bowl and take the rest of the ingredients in it and mix them well. When the ingredients are mixed well, take the mixture and pour it over the bowl of cabbages and collard leaves, and coat them all properly. Thus it is ready to be served. Enjoy!!

Tomato mozzarella salad

Ingredients

5 Tomatoes
1 cup Mozzarella cheese, cut in slices
2 tbsp. Olive oil

2 tbsp. Balsamic vinegar
Salt and pepper to taste
Fresh leaves of basil, torn in pieces

Method

Take the tomatoes and mozzarellas on a serving dish and place them in an alternate manner. Now the oil, vinegar, salt and the pepper are to be mixed and then are to be poured over the serving dish. Before serving the salad, sprinkle the basil leaves over the salad. Enjoy!!

BLT salad

Ingredients

1 pound of bacon
1 cup of mayonnaise
1 tsp. Garlic powder
Salt and pepper, to taste

1 head Romaine
2Tomatoes
2 Croutons

Method

The bacons are to be cook in a pan over a medium heat until they are evenly browned in color and then drain them and set at a side. Now take a food processor and process the mayonnaise, milk, garlic powder, pepper, until they are smooth in texture. Thus the dressing of the salad is ready. Now toss the lettuce, cooked bacons, tomatoes and croutons in a bowl and then pour the dressing and coat them properly. Before serving cool it for an hour or two. Enjoy!!

Beautiful salad

Ingredients

1 bunch Baby spinach leaves
2 Red onions
1 can of mandarin oranges, drained

1 cup Cranberries, dried
½ cup Feta cheese, crumbled
1 cup of vinaigrette salad dressing mix

Method

Take all the ingredients except the salad dressing mix, to a large sized bowl and mix them well. When the ingredients are properly mixed, sprinkle the salad dressing mix over the bowl of salad and thus the beautiful salad is ready to be served. Enjoy!!

Almond mandarin salad

Ingredients

1/2 pound of bacon
2 tsp. White wine vinegar
1 tsp. Honey
1 tsp. Hot mustard
1 tsp. Celery salt

1 tsp. Paprika
1 Red leaf lettuce
1 can of mandarin oranges, drained
2 Green onions, cut in wedges
1 cup of almond, silvered

Method

Take a pan and cook the bacon, covering them, until they turn brown in color. For preparing the salad dressing, blend the honey, vinegar, mustard with the celery salt, paprika and olive oil. Now the lettuce, oranges, cooked bacons and the silvered almonds are to be tossed in to a bowl and then pour the salad dressing over it and mix them well so that they are well coated. Before serving the salad, let them cool for an hour. Enjoy!!

Tuna and mandarin salad

Ingredients

Olive oil
1 can of tuna
1 pack of mixed baby greens

1 granny smith apple, peeled and chopped
1 can of mandarin oranges

Method

The olive oil is to be heated and the tuna is to be sautéed until cooked completely.

Now take a bowl and toss the salad greens with the sautéed tuna, apples and the oranges. Thus, the salad is ready to be served. Enjoy!!

Macaroni and tuna fish salad

Ingredients

1 packet of macaroni
2 cans of tuna
1 cup mayonnaise
Salt and pepper, to taste

1 pinch Garlic powder
1 pinch of oregano, dried
1 Onion, finely shredded

Method

Take salted water to a pot and bring it to boil and then add the macaroni and cook them, after cooking them drain the macaroni and then cool it. Now the cans of tuna are to be mixed with the cooked macaroni and then add the mayonnaise to it and mix them well. Now add the rest of the ingredients to the mixture and mix them well. When all the ingredients are mixed, let them cool for about an hour or two. Thus the delicious tuna fish salad is ready to be served. Enjoy!!

Asian salad

Ingredients

2 pack of ramen noodles
1 cup of almonds, blanched and silvered
2 tsp. Sesame seeds
1/2 cup of butter
1 head of Napa cabbage, chopped

1 bunch of green onions, chopped
¼ cup Vegetable oil
2-3 tsp. White sugar
2 tsp. Soy sauce

Method

Take a pan and heat the butter or margarine and then pour the ramen noodles, sesame seeds and almonds in it over low heat and cook them, until they are browned. When cooked, let them cool. Now take a small sized pan and pour the vegetable oil, sugar and vinegar and then bring them to boil for about a minute and then cool it and when cooled, add the soy sauce in it. Take a bowl and then mix all the ingredients along with the cooked ramen noodles and the sugar mixture and then toss them well. Before serving the salad, let it cool for an hour or more. Enjoy!!

Asian chicken pasta salad

Ingredients

1 packet Rotelle pasta
2 Chicken breasts, boneless, cut in pieces, cooked
2-3 tbsp. Vegetable oil
Salt
2-3 carrots, shredded

1/2 pound of mushrooms
1/2 head of broccoli
1/2 head of cauliflower
Water
2 tsp. Soy sauce
2 tsp. Sesame oil

Method

Take salted water in a pot and bring it to boil, now add the pack of pasta in it and cook them. When cooked, drain the pasta and set aside. Now take a pan and cook the carrots with salt until they are crispy and tender. Now take a bowl and add the pasta, carrots with chicken breasts and mix them well. Now cook the mushrooms and take it to the bowl and then add the rest of the ingredients to it and mix well. Serve the salad chilled. Enjoy!!

Cobb salad

Ingredients

4-5 Bacon slices 2 Eggs
1 head Iceberg lettuce
1 Chicken breast
2 Tomatoes, sliced

¼ cup Blue cheese, shredded
2 Green onions, sliced
A bottle of salad dressing

Method

Boil the eggs, peel and chop. Pan fry the bacon and chicken, separately until browned. Crumble. Just before serving, combine all the ingredients in a large mixing bowl and mix well. Serve without delay. Enjoy!!

Arugula Corn Salad with Bacon Recipe

Ingredients

4 large corns
2 cups of chopped arugula
4 strips of bacon
1/3 cup of chopped green onions

1 tbsp. olive oil
1 tbsp. wine vinegar
1/8 tsp. cumin
Salt and black pepper

Method

Heat the corn, in their husks, also on the grill for a smoky flavor, for 12-15 minutes. In a medium sized basin, combine the corn, arugula, bacon, and onions. In a separate basin, beat the vinegar, oil, salt and pepper. Mix covering into salad just before serving and serve without delay. Enjoy!

Black Eyed Pea Salad Recipe

Ingredients

2 cups of dry black-eyed peas
230grams feta cheese
230grams of sun-dried tomatoes
1 cup Kalamata black olives

Finely chopped green onion
Chopped garlic clove
1 large bunch of chopped spinach
Juice and Zest of a lemon

Method

Cook the peas in salinated water until just done. Drain and wash with cold water. In a bowl mix all the ingredients except for the lemon juice. Add the lemon juice just before serving and serve immediately. Enjoy!

Arugula Salad with Beets and Goat Cheese Recipe

Ingredients

Salad Ingredients:
2 Peeled Beets
Handful of Arugula leaves
½ cup Goat cheese, crumbled
½ cup Walnuts, chopped
Dressing Ingredients:

¼ cup Olive oil
½ Lemon
¼ tsp. Dry powdered mustard
¾ tsp. Sugar
Salt and pepper

Method

For the dressing combine together the ¼ tsp. of powdered mustard, ¾ tsp. of sugar, ½ lemon, and ¼ cup of olive oil, salt and pepper to flavor. Combine a handful of arugula leaves, a few beet juliennes, crumbled goat cheese and chopped walnuts. Top with the dressing just before serving. Serve without delay. Enjoy!

Asian Coleslaw Recipe

Ingredients

1 cup Creamy peanut butter
6 tbsp. vegetable oil
½ tsp. toasted sesame oil
4 tbsp. seasoned rice vinegar

4 cups of thinly sliced cabbage
½ cup grated carrots
¼ cup toasted peeled peanuts

Method

Add peanut butter in an average basin and add the toasted sesame oil and beat until nicely softly. Toast the peanuts to get even better flavor with just a minute toasting. Transfer peanuts from pan to a huge bowl. Toss the carrots, cabbage and peanuts together, and any other ingredients you care to add and Serve without delay. Enjoy!

Asian Noodle Salad Recipe

Ingredients

280grams Chinese noodles
1/3 cup soy sauce
3 cups of broccoli florets
115 grams green gram bean sprouts

3 thinly sliced onions,
1 red bell pepper
1/4 thinly sliced bulky cabbage
1 huge peeled carrot

Method

Pour 4 glasses of water into huge pot, add Chinese noodles. Mix the noodles constantly while they cook. Ensure you follow the noodle package instructions, if using Chinese noodles, they should be done after 5minutes of cooking. Drain noodles, wash with cold water to stop the cooking, extend the noodles out on a sheet pan to air dry. Add broccoli florets and sufficient water to come up to the level of the steamer. Cover and steam cook for 4 minutes. Combine all the ingredients in a bowl. Serve without delay. Enjoy!

Asparagus Artichoke Salad Recipe

Ingredients

1 large thinly sliced onion
3 tbsp. lemon juice
450grams thick asparagus
2 tbsp. olive oil

1 tsp. garlic powder
1 pint grape

Method

First immerse the sliced onions in the lemon juice, and roast the asparagus in a preheated oven at 400 degrees F. For the asparagus spears add 1 tbsp. of olive oil, and salt them well. Place in a single layer in a foil-lined roasting saucepan and cook for 10 minutes until lightly browned. To grill the asparagus, organize your charcoal grill at high temperature, between 5 to 10 minutes. Remove the asparagus from the grill and cut into bite pieces, set the asparagus and all ingredients into a huge bowl and blend to combine and Serve without delay. Enjoy!

Asparagus Salad with Shrimp Recipe

Ingredients

450grams asparagus
226grams pink salad shrimp
¼ cup of extra-virgin olive oil
1 minced garlic clove

1 tbsp. lemon juice
1 tbsp. minced parsley
Salt and black pepper

Method

Bring an average pot of water to a boil. Add the asparagus to the boiling water and boil for 3 minutes. If they are pre-cooked, remove after 30 seconds. If the shrimps are raw, boil them for 3 minutes, until cooked through. Remove the shrimp and add them to a huge bowl. Slice the asparagus spears finely diagonally. Slash the asparagus tips off in one piece. Add the remaining ingredients and toss to combine. Add salt and black pepper to taste. Add more lemon juice if desired, to taste and Serve without delay. Enjoy!

Blueberry Peach Fruit Salad with Thyme Recipe

Ingredients

4 peaches
4 nectarines
1 cup of blueberries
2 tsp. of chopped thyme fresh
1 tsp. of ginger, grated

¼ cup of lemon juice
1 tsp. of lemon zest
1/2 cup of water
¼ cup of sugar

Method

Place the water and sugar into a saucepot and heat to a simmer and cook liquid is reduced by half into simple syrup, allow to cool. Chop up the nectarines and peaches and Add them in a basin with the blueberries. Pour over the cooled syrup. Add the lemon zest, thyme, lemon juice, and ginger. Blend and cover up with plastic wrap, place in the refrigerator and allow macerating for one hour. Serve without delay. Enjoy!

Broccoli Salad Recipe

Ingredients

salt
6 cups broccoli florets
1/2 cup of toasted almonds
1/2 cup cooked bacon
¼ cup of chopped onion

1 cup of thawed frozen peas
1 cup of mayonnaise
apple cider vinegar
¼ cup of honey

Method

Bring a huge pot of water, salted with a tsp. of salt, to a simmer. Add the broccoli florets. Cook 2 minutes, depending on how crispy you want the broccoli. 1 minute will turn the broccoli bright greenish color, and leave it still pretty crispy. Set your regulator and do not cook for more than 2 minutes. Combine broccoli florets, crumbled bacon, almonds, chopped onion, and peas in a huge serving basin in a separate pudding basin, beat together mayonnaise, vinegar and honey and flip to blend well, Chill thoroughly before. Serve without delay. Enjoy!

Broccoli Slaw with Cranberry Orange Dressing Recipe

Ingredients

2 tbsp. balsamic vinegar
½ cup dried sweetened cranberries
2 tsp. whole grain mustard
2 tbsp. red wine vinegar
1 clove garlic
½ cup orange juice
2-3 slices orange zest

Kosher salt
6 tbsp. vegetable oil
¼ cup of mayonnaise
½ head cabbage
2-3 green onions
¼ cup dried cranberries
2-3 slices grated orange zest

Method

Add the red wine vinegar and balsamic vinegar, mustard, plumped dried cranberries, honey, garlic, orange juice, orange zest, and salt into a food processor and pulsate until pureed soft. Gradually add the vegetable oil, while blending, to form a good mixture. Then add the mayonnaise and pulse until combined. Add grated broccoli stalks, carrots, dried cranberries, orange zest, and kosher salt into a mixing bowl.

Add the dressing and toss to combine, until the dressing is evenly distributed. Serve without delay. Enjoy!

Avocado Salad with Heirloom Tomatoes

Ingredients

1 1/2 sliced and peeled avocados
1 1/2 tomatoes, sliced
2 Sliced green onions or chopped fresh

chives
Lemon Juice from one slice
A pinch of coarse salt

Method

Arrange slices of avocado and tomato on a plate. Drizzle lemon juice over chives, and coarse salt. Remove the pit from one half of an avocado still in its skin, and remove its pulp in a bowl. Add in the tomato and prepared chives and mix well. Serve without delay. Enjoy!

Cardamom Citrus Fruit Salad Recipe

Ingredients

1 huge ruby pink grape fruit
3 combination of navel oranges or navel oranges a mandarin oranges, blood oranges and or tangerines

¼ cup of honey
2 tbsp. fresh lemon or lime juice
1/4 tsp. of ground cardamom

Method

First unpeel the fruit, cut away the membranes of the segments with a sharp knife. Bring together the peeled segments in an addition bowl. Conduit off any surplus juice from the fruit into diminutive saucepan. Add the honey, lime juice and cardamom to the saucepan. Boil for 10 minutes and then remove from heat and let chill to room temperature. Let stand for 15 minutes or put on ice until ready. Serve without delay. Enjoy!

Capers Corn Salad Recipe

Ingredients

6 ears of sweet corn
¼ cup of olive oil
sherry vinegar

black pepper
1 ½ tsp. kosher salt
½ tsp. sugar

3 chopped seeded tomatoes
½ cup sliced scallions

230grams fresh mozzarella
basil leaves

Method

Arrange your grill on high heat, and place the corn cobs in their husks directly on the grill. Cook for 15 minutes, there is no need to immerse the corn in water first if the corn is fresh. If you want some burn on the corn itself, remove a few of the outer corn husks first, so there is less of a caring layer around the corn. Take a huge bowl, and flip together the corn, Mozzarella, scallions, tomatoes, and the dressing. Right before serving, stir in the freshly sliced basil. Serve without delay. Enjoy!

Celery Root Salad

Ingredients

½ cup mayonnaise
2 tbsp. mustard, Dijon
1 tbsp. lemon juice
2 tbsp. parsley, chopped
545gm celery root equally quartered,

peeled & coarsely grated just before mixing
½ tart green apple, peeled, cored, julienned
Salt and ground pepper

Method

Combine mayonnaise with mustard along with lemon juice and parsley in a bowl. Crinkle celery root with apple and season with salt & pepper, wrap it up and refrigerate until cooled, 1 hour minimum . Enjoy!

Cherry Tomato Cucumber Feta Salad

Ingredients

2 or 3 cups of cherry tomatoes, sliced into two halves
1 cup chopped cucumber, peeled
1/4 cup crumbled cheese, feta
1 tbsp. mint chiffonaded leaves
1 tbsp. oregano, fresh, chopped

1 tbsp. lemon juice
2 tbsp. shallots or green onions, finely chopped
2 tbsp. olive oil
Salt(Coarse and black pepper, freshly ground to taste

Method

Softly toss the cherry tomatoes along with cucumber, cheese, onions, mint & oregano together. Garnish with lemon juice and salt & pepper along with olive oil. Enjoy!

Cucumber Salad with Mint and Feta Recipe

Ingredients

453 grams cucumbers, thinly sliced
¼ thinly sliced red onion, and cut into
1-inch extensive segments
2 - 3 thinly sliced red radishes
10 thinly sliced mint leaves

White vinegar
Olive oil
¼ of pound feta cheese
freshly ground pepper and Salt

Method

In an average sized mixing bowl, smoothly mix the sliced cucumbers, mint leaves, radishes, red onion with a diminutive bit of white vinegar and olive oil, salt and freshly ground pepper to flavor. Just before serving, shake over on crumbled bits of feta cheese. Serve immediately before any delay. Enjoy!

Cherry Tomato Orzo Salad Recipe

Ingredients

230 grams orzo pasta
Salt and Black pepper to taste
1 pint sliced in half red cherry tomatoes
1 pint sliced in half yellow cherry tomatoes
¼ cup of olive oil

230 grams crumbled feta cheese
1 huge chopped and peeled cucumber
2 green thinly sliced onions
fresh minced oregano,

Method

Fill a big pot with water and bring to a boil. Add the orzo, stirring it so that it doesn't stick to the bottom of the pan. Cook, at a high boil until al dente, ripe through, but still a bit resolute. Mix with the rest of the ingredients, the tomatoes, oregano, feta cheese, green onions, cucumber and black pepper. Serve without delay. Enjoy!

Cucumber Salad with Grapes and Almonds Recipe

Ingredients

¼ cup slivered almonds
1 pound peeled cucumbers
salt
1 tsp. garlic, minced
20 sliced green grapes

2 tbsp. olive oil
1 sherry or white wine vinegar
2 tsp. minced chives, for garnish

Method

Slice the cucumbers lengthwise. Use a spoon to scoop out the seeds in the middle, discard the seeds. If using slightly big cucumbers, sliver them again lengthwise. Mix around to coat the salt evenly on the cucumber. Toast the sliced almonds in a small pan on simmering heat, flipping them often, remove in a bowl to cool. Mix the almonds, cucumbers, grapes, garlic, olive oil, and vinegar together in a big bowl and add more salt to taste. Garnish with chives and serve without delay. Enjoy!

Cucumber Mint Quinoa Salad Recipe

Ingredients

1 cup quinoa
2 cups of water
½ tsp. kosher salt
1 large peeled cucumber
¼ cup thinly sliced mint

1 thinly sliced green onion
4 tbsp. rice vinegar
olive oil
1 peeled avocado

Method

Place the quinoa in a medium sized saucepan, pour in water. Add half a tsp. of salt, diminish to a low heat. Let the cooked quinoa cool to room temperature. You can cool down the quinoa speedily by spreading it out on a sheet pan. Cut the cucumber in long slices. Shake over with seasoned rice vinegar and flip again. Smoothly fold in chop up avocado if using and serve without delay. Enjoy!

Couscous with Pistachios and Apricots Recipe

Ingredients

½ cup chopped red onion
¼ cup lemon juice
1 box of couscous
2 tbsp. olive oil

½ cup raw pistachios
10 dried chopped apricots
1/3 cup chopped parsley

Method

Put the chopped onion in a little bowl. Empty the lemon juice over the onions set aside and let the onions soak in the lemon juice. Toast the pistachios in a tiny pan on simmering heat until they brown. Put 2 cups of water in a medium saucepan and bring to a boil. Add a tbsp. of olive oil and one tsp. of salt to the water; add the couscous and cook covered for 5-6 minutes. Stir in the pistachios, chopped apricots and parsley. Mix in the red onion and lemon juice. Serve without delay. Enjoy!

Coleslaw Recipe

Ingredients

½ Cabbage, sliced
½ Carrot, sliced
2 – 3 Green onions, sliced
3 tbsp. Mayonnaise

½ tsp. Yellow mustard
2 tbsp. Rice vinegar
Sugar, to taste
Salt and pepper, to taste

Method

Combine all the sliced vegetables in a bowl. To make the dressing, mix together the mayonnaise, yellow mustard and rice vinegar. Just before serving, drizzle the dressing on the veggies and sprinkle with some salt, pepper and sugar. Serve without delay. Enjoy!

Cold Pea Salad Recipe

Ingredients

453 grams frozen petite peas, do not thaw
170 grams smokehouse almonds, chopped, rinsed to take off the excess salt, preferably by hand
½ cup of chopped green onions

230 grams chopped water chestnuts
2/3 cup of mayonnaise
2 tbsp. yellow curry powder
Salt to taste
Pepper to taste

Method

Combine the frozen green onions, peas, almonds, and water chestnuts. Combine together the mayonnaise and curry powder in a separate mixing bowl. Smoothly fold the mayonnaise combination into peas. Sprinkle salt and freshly ground black pepper to flavor. Serve without delay. Enjoy!

Cucumber Yogurt Salad Recipe

Ingredients

2 peeled then sliced cucumbers, quartered lengthwise
1 cup Plain yogurt
1 tsp. a couple of tsps., or dried dill of fresh dill
Salt to taste

Pepper to taste

Method

First taste the cucumbers to make sure that they are not sour. If the cucumber is sour, soak the cucumber slices in salted water for half an hour, or longer, until the bitterness is lost, then rinse and drain before using. To prepare the salad, simply gently combine together the ingredients. Shake over or sprinkle of salt and sprinkle pepper as for flavor. Serve without delay. Enjoy!

Dad's Greek Salad Recipe

Ingredients

6 tbsp. olive oil
2 tbsp. fresh lemon juice
½ tsp. fresh chopped garlic
4 tablespoons red wine vinegar
½ tsp. dried oregano
½ tsp. dill weed
Salt and freshly ground black pepper

3 bulky seeded plum tomatoes
¾ peeled, coarsely chopped cucumber
½ peeled and chopped red onion
1 bell coarsely chopped pepper
½ cup of chopped pitted black olives
A heaping 1/2 cup crumbled feta cheese

Method

Mix up the vinegar, olive oil, garlic, lemon juice, oregano and dill weed together until blended. Season to taste with salt and freshly ground black pepper. Combine the tomatoes, along with cucumber, onion, bell pepper, olives in a bowl. Sprinkle cheese over and Serve without delay. Enjoy!

Dad's Potato Salad Recipe

Ingredients

4 peeled midsized Russet potatoes
4 tbsp. juice from kosher dill pickles
3 tbsp. finely chopped dill pickles
¼ cup chopped parsley
½ cup chopped red onion
2 stalks celery

2 chopped scallions
½ cup mayonnaise
2 tsp. Dijon mustard
Kosher salt and ground black pepper to flavor

Method

Put peeled, cut potatoes in a huge pot. Cover with an inch of salted water. Place the pot of water to boil. Simmer for 20 minutes until just fork tender. Remove from pot, let cool until warm. Add celery, parsley, scallions and, the hardboiled egg, carrots, and red bell pepper. Part little basin, blend mayonnaise with mustard. Sprinkle salt and pepper to taste. Serve without delay. Enjoy!

Endive Salad with Walnuts, Pears, and Gorgonzola Recipe

Ingredients

3 sliced first lengthwise Endive heads, then crosswise in ½ inch slices
2 tbsp. chopped walnuts
2 tbsp. crumbled gorgonzola
1 cored and chopped Bartlett pear,

2 tbsp. olive oil
2 tsp. cider vinegar
Sprinkle of kosher salt and freshly ground black pepper

Method

Put the chopped endive in a huge bowl. Add the crumbled gorgonzola, walnuts, and chopped pears, chop the pears and walnuts more finely. Flip to combine, drizzle olive over the salad with some crumbled blue cheese in the endive leaves, like filling little boats, for appetizers. Sprinkle cider vinegar over the salad. Toss to combine. Season to taste with a shake over of salt and pepper. Serve without delay. Enjoy!

Fennel Slaw with Mint Vinaigrette Recipe Ingredients

1 huge fennel bulb
1 ½ tsp. sugar
2 lemon juice
¼ cup olive oil

½ tsp. mustard
½ tsp. salt
1 bunch chopped fresh mint
2 minced shallot

Method

Put together the vinaigrette. Place the lemon juice, onions, salt, mustard, sugar and mint in a mixer and pulse briefly to combine. With the motor running, mix in the olive oil until it is well combined. Using a mandolin, shave the fennel into 1/8 inch piece starting from the bottom of the bulb. Don't worry about coring the fennel bulb, it's preventable. If you don't have a mandolin, slice the bulb as thin as you can. Cut some of the fennel fronds as well to flip in with the salad. Serve without delay. Enjoy!

Fennel, Radicchio and Endive Salad Recipe

Ingredients

Salad
1 head radicchio
3 Belgian endives
1 huge fennel bulb

1 cup coarsely grated parmesan cheese
Dressing
3 tbsp. fennel fronds
½ tsp. mustard

3 tsp. minced onion
2 tbsp. lemon juice
1 tsp. salt

1 tsp. sugar
1/3 cup olive oil

Method

Cut the head of radicchio in half, then in quarters. Take each quarter and cut slices of about half inch thick crosswise on the radicchio from the end toward the core. Cut thin slices from each quarter toward the core. Toss all the cut vegetables in a huge bowl with the grated parmesan. Add in the lemon juice, mustard, onion, salt and sugar. Drizzle the olive oil and puree the dressing for 45 second. Serve without delay. Enjoy!

Festive Beet Citrus Salad with Kale and Pistachios Recipe

Ingredients

10 mix of red beets
3 blood oranges
1 bunch of thinly sliced kale
1 cup roughly chopped roasted pistachios
¼ cup chopped mint leaves
3 chopped Italian parsley

Dressing:
2 tbsp. lemon juice
1/2 cup quality extra virgin olive oil
2 coarsely chopped capers
Salt and pepper to flavor

Method

Cook the beets separately by color. Place each batch of beets in a vessel and cover with about an inch of water. Add in some tsp. of salt. While the beets are cook, organize the dressing. Place all of the dressing ingredients into a container and shake until well mix together. Prepare salad by placing the beets, parsley, over the kale, sprinkling with the chopped roasted pistachios. Serve topped with the prepared dressing. Enjoy!

Golden Beet and Pomegranate Salad Recipe

Ingredients

3 golden haired beets
1 cup chopped red onion
¼ cup red wine vinegar
¼ cup chicken broth

1 cup of sugar
½ tsp. grated orange peel
¼ cup pomegranate seeds

Method

Cook the beets and roast them at 375 degrees F for an hour and allow to cool. Unpeel and chop into half inch cubes. In a medium sized skillet over high heat, onion, vinegar, broth, sugar, and orange peel and bring to a boil, stirring often, until liquid is reduced to tbsp., about 5 minutes. Mix pomegranate seeds into the beet combination and salt to flavor. Serve without delay. Enjoy!

Delicious Corn and Black Bean Salad

Ingredients

1 tbsp. plus 3 tbsp. olive oil
1/2 onion, chopped
1 cup corn kernels, from about 2 ears of corn
12 tbsp. chopped cilantro
1 15 1/2-oz. can black beans, drained and

rinsed
1½ tomatoes, about 0.5 lbs., cored, seeded and chopped
1½ tbsp. red wine vinegar
1 tsp. Dijon mustard
Salt and pepper

Method

Keep your oven to preheat to 400 degrees F. Place 1 tbsp. oil in an ovenproof skillet and heat on high. Sauté the onions until tender. Add in the corn kernels and keep stirring until soft. Place the skillet in the preheated oven and broil until the vegetables are brown, stirring often. This will take about 20 minutes. Immediately remove in a plate and allow to cool. Place the cooled corn mix in a bowl and add in the tomatoes, cilantro and beans and mix well. In a small bowl pour in the vinegar, mustard, pepper and salt and mix well until the salt dissolves. Slowly add in the 3 tbsp. oil and keep whisking until all the ingredients are well incorporated. Pour this dressing over the corn mix and serve immediately. Enjoy!

Crispy Broccoli Slaw

Ingredients

4 slices bacon
1/2 large head broccoli
1/2 small red onion, minced, 1/2 cup
3 tbsp. golden raisins

3 tbsp. mayonnaise
1½ tbsp. white balsamic vinegar
2 tbsp. honey
Salt and pepper

Method

Brown the bacon slices in a skillet until crisp. Drain it on a kitchen towel and crumble it into half inch pieces. Keep aside. Separate the florets from the broccoli and chop the stem into bite sized pieces. Place in a large bowl and mix together with the raisins and onion. In another bowl combine the vinegar and mayonnaise and mix until smooth. Pour in the honey and season with salt and pepper. Just before serving pour the dressing over the broccoli mix and toss to coat. Top with the crumbled bacon and serve immediately.   Enjoy!

Bistro-Style Salad

Ingredients

1 ½ tbsp. finely chopped walnuts
2 large eggs
Cooking spray
1 bacon slice, uncooked
4 cups gourmet salad greens
2 tbsp., 0.5 ounce crumbled blue cheese
1/2 Bartlett pear, cored and thinly sliced

½ tbsp. white wine vinegar
1/2 tbsp. extra virgin olive oil
1/4 tsp. dried tarragon
1/4 tsp. Dijon mustard
2, 1-inch-thick slices French bread baguette, toasted

Method

Roast the walnuts in a small skillet until an aroma fills the kitchen. This should take about 3-4 minutes when cooking on high heat. Remove and keep aside. Spray 2 6 ounce custard cups with the cooking spray. Break an egg in each custard cup. Using a plastic wrap cover them both and microwave on high for 40 seconds or until the eggs are set. Set aside for 1 minute and remove on a paper towel. Brown the bacon in a skillet until crisp. Drain and crumble. Reserve the fat. In a large bowl mix together the crumbled bacon, roasted walnuts, salad greens, blue cheese and pear. In another small bowl combine about 1 tsp. of fat, vinegar, oil, tarragon and mustard and whisk until combined. Just before serving drizzle the dressing over the salad and serve topped with the egg and French baguette on the side. Enjoy!

Delicious Chicken Salad

Ingredients

2 tbsp. fat-free, less-sodium chicken broth
1 tbsp. rice wine vinegar
1/2 tbsp. Thai fish sauce
1/2 tbsp. low-sodium soy sauce
1/2 tbsp. garlic, chopped
1 tsp. sugar
1/2 pound chicken breast tenders, skinless, boneless, cut into bite sized pieces
1/2 tbsp. peanut oil

2 cups mixed salad greens
2 tbsp. fresh basil, chopped
2 tbsp. red onion, thinly sliced
1 tbsp. dry-roasted peanuts finely chopped unsalted
Lime wedges, optional

Method

In a medium sized bowl combine the chicken broth, rice wine vinegar, Thai fish sauce, low-sodium soy sauce, garlic and sugar. Put the chicken pieces in this marinade and coat the chicken in the mix and keep aside for a few minutes. Add the oil in a large skillet and heat on medium heat. Remove the pieces of chicken from the marinade and cook in the heated pan for about 4-5 minutes or until cooked completely. Pour in the marinade and cook on a reduced flame until the gravy thickens. Remove from heat. In a large bowl mix together the greens, basil and chicken and toss well until coated. Serve the salad topped with the onion and peanuts with lemon wedges on the side. Enjoy!

Healthy Vegetable & Soba Noodle Salad

Ingredients

2, 8-ounce packages soba noodles
2 ½ cups frozen green soybeans
1 ½ cups carrots, julienned
2/3 cup green onions, sliced
4 tbsp. fresh cilantro, chopped
3 tsp. serrano chili, chopped
2 pound shrimp, peeled and deveined
1/2 tsp. salt

1/2 tsp. black pepper
Cooking spray
2 tbsp. fresh orange juice
2 tbsp. fresh lime juice
1 tbsp. low-sodium soy sauce
1 tbsp. dark sesame oil
1 tbsp. olive oil

Method

Boil a pot of water and cook the noodles in it until almost done. In a pan cook the soybeans for 1 minute or until really hot. Remove from pan and drain. Mix together the noodles with the carrots, onions, cilantro and chili. Spray a large skillet with some cooking spray and heat on a medium flame. Toss the shrimp with salt and pepper. Place the shrimp in the pan and cook until done. Add the shrimp to the noodle mix. In a small bowl add the orange juice and the other ingredients to it and mix well. Pour the dressing over the noodle mix and toss well until coated. Enjoy!

Lettuce and Watercress Salad with an Anchovy Dressing

Ingredients

Dressing:
1 cup plain fat-free yogurt
1/2 cup reduced-fat mayonnaise
4 tbsp. chopped fresh flat-leaf parsley

6 tbsp. chopped green onions
2 tbsp. chopped fresh chives
6 tbsp. white wine vinegar
4 tsp. anchovy paste

2 tsp. chopped fresh tarragon
1/2 tsp. freshly ground black pepper
1/4 tsp. salt
2 garlic cloves, minced
Salad:
16 cups torn romaine lettuce
2 cup trimmed watercress
3 cups chopped cooked chicken breast

4 tomatoes, each cut into 8 wedges, about 1 pound
4 hard-cooked large eggs, each cut into 4 wedges
1 cup diced peeled avocado
1/2 cup, 1 1/2 ounces crumbled blue cheese

Method

Put all the ingredients required for the dressing in a food processor and give it a whirl and blend until smooth. Refrigerate. In a large bowl place all the ingredients for the salad and toss well. Pour over the dressing just before serving. Enjoy!

Prosciutto Topped Chicken Salad

Ingredients

1, 1-ounce slices sourdough bread, cut into 1/2-inch cubes
Cooking spray
1/4 tsp. dried basil
1 pinch garlic powder
1 ½ tbsp. extra-virgin olive oil, divided
1 ounce very thin slices prosciutto, chopped

1 tbsp. fresh lemon juice
1/8 tsp. salt
1, 5-ounce packages baby arugula
3/4 ounces Asiago cheese, shaved and divided, about 1/3 cup
3 ounces shredded skinless, boneless rotisserie chicken breast
1/2 cup grape tomatoes, halved

Method

Keep your oven to preheat on 425 degrees F. Lightly grease a baking sheet with some cooking spray and place the bread cubes on it in a single layer. Sprinkle the garlic powder and add the basil and mix well. Pop into preheated oven and bake for 10 minutes or until the bread is crisp. In a large nonstick skillet add some oil and sauté the prosciutto until crisp. Remove from the pan and drain. Mix the remaining oil, lemon juice and salt in a bowl. In a large bowl place the arugula, half the cheese, and juice mix and toss well. While serving top the salad with the chicken, crisp prosciutto, tomatoes, the remaining cheese and croutons and mix and serve. Enjoy!

Delicious Shrimp Topped Arugula Salad

Ingredients

2 cups loosely packed baby arugula
1/2 cup red bell pepper, julienned
1/4 cup carrot, julienned
1 1/2 tbsp. extra-virgin olive oil, divided
1 tsp. minced fresh rosemary

1/4 tsp. crushed red pepper
1 garlic cloves, thinly sliced
8 large shrimp, peeled and deveined
1 1/2 tbsp. white balsamic vinegar

Method

In a large bowl mix together the baby arugula, red bell pepper and carrots. In a large skillet add about 1 tbsp. of oil and heat it on medium heat. Place the pepper, garlic and rosemary in the pan and cook until the garlic softens. Add the shrimp and increase the heat. Cook until the shrimp is cooked. Place the shrimp in a bowl. In the pan add the remaining oil and vinegar and heat until warm. Pour this mix on the arugula mixture and toss until the dressing coats the vegetables. Top the salad with the shrimp and serve immediately. Enjoy!

Shrimp Cobb Salad

Ingredients

2 slices center-cut bacon
1/2 pound large shrimp, peeled and deveined
1/4 tsp. paprika
1/8 tsp. black pepper
Cooking spray
1/8 tsp. salt, divided
1 1/4 tbsp. fresh lemon juice

3/4 tbsp. extra-virgin olive oil
1/4 tsp. whole-grain Dijon mustard
1/2, 10-ounce package romaine salad
1 cup cherry tomatoes, quartered
1/2 cup shredded carrots
1/2 cup frozen whole-kernel corn, thawed
1/2 ripe peeled avocado, cut into 4 wedges

Method

Brown the bacon in a pan until crisp. Cut lengthwise. Clean the pan and spray it with cooking spray. Place the pan on the stove again and heat on medium heat. Toss the shrimp with some pepper and paprika. Add the shrimp to the pan and cook until ready. Sprinkle some salt and mix well. In a small bowl combine the lemon juice, oil, salt and mustard together in a bowl. Mix together the lettuce, shrimp, tomatoes, carrot, corn, avocado and bacon in a bowl and drizzle the dressing over it. Toss well and serve immediately. Enjoy!

Melon and Prosciutto Salad

Ingredients

1 1/2 cups, 1/2-inch cubed honeydew melon

1 1/2 cups, 1/2-inch cubed cantaloupe

1 tbsp. thinly sliced fresh mint

1/2 tsp. fresh lemon juice

1/8 tsp. freshly ground black pepper

1 ounces thinly sliced prosciutto, cut into thin strips

1/4 cup, 2 ounces shaved fresh Parmigiano-Reggiano cheese

Cracked black pepper, optional

Mint sprigs, optional

Method

Combine all the ingredients together in a large mixing bowl and toss well until well-coated. Serve garnished with some pepper and mint sprigs. Serve immediately. Enjoy!

Corn and White Bean Salad

Ingredients

1 head escarole, quartered lengthwise and rinsed

Cooking spray

1 ounce pancetta, chopped

1/2 medium zucchini, quartered and cut into julienne strips

1/2 garlic clove, minced

1/2 cup fresh corn kernels

1/4 cup chopped fresh flat-leaf parsley

1/2, 15-ounce can navy beans, rinsed and drained

1 tbsp. red wine vinegar

1/2 tsp. extra virgin olive oil

1/4 tsp. black pepper

Method

Cook the escarole in a large skillet on medium heat for 3 minutes or until it starts wilting around the edges. Wipe the pan and coat it with some cooking spray. Heat it on a medium high flame and add the pancetta, zucchini and garlic to it and sauté until they are tender. Add in the corn and cook for another minute. Combine the corn mixture and escarole in a large bowl. Add in the parsley and vinegar and mix well. Add in the remaining ingredients and toss well. Serve. Enjoy!

Thai Style Shrimp Salad

Ingredients

2 ounces uncooked linguine

6 ounces peeled and deveined medium

shrimp

1/4 cup fresh lime juice

1/2 tbsp. sugar
1/2 tbsp. Sriracha, hot chili sauce, such as
Huy Fong
1/2 tsp. fish sauce
2 cups torn romaine lettuce
3/4 cup red onion, vertically sliced

1/8 cup carrots, julienned
1/4 cup chopped fresh mint leaves
1/8 cup chopped fresh cilantro
3 tbsp. chopped dry-roasted cashews,
unsalted

Method

Prepare the pasta according to the instructions on the packet. When the pasta is almost cooked add in the shrimp and cook for 3 minutes. Drain and place in a colander. Run some cold water on it. In a bowl combine the lemon juice, sugar, Sriracha and fish sauce. Mix until the sugar dissolves. Add in all the ingredients except for the cashews. Toss well. Top with cashews and serve immediately. Enjoy!

Delicious Salad with Spicy Pineapple Dressing

Ingredients

1/2 pound skinless, boneless chicken
breast
1/2 tsp. chili powder
1/4 tsp. salt
Cooking spray
3/4 cup, 1-inch cubed fresh pineapple,
about 8 ounces , divided
1 tbsp. chopped fresh cilantro
1 tbsp. fresh orange juice

2 tsp. apple cider vinegar
1/4 tsp. minced habanero pepper
1/2 large garlic clove
1/8 cup extra-virgin olive oil
1/2 cup jicama, peeled and julienned
1/3 cup thinly sliced red bell pepper
1/4 cup thinly sliced red onion
1/2, 5-ounce package fresh baby spinach,
about 4 cups

Method

Pound the chicken to an even thickness and sprinkle with salt and chili powder. Spray some cooking spray on the chicken and place on a preheated grill and cook until the chicken is ready. Keep aside. Place half the pineapple, orange juice, cilantro, habanero, garlic and vinegar in a blender and blend until smooth. Slowly trickle in the olive oil and keep blending until combined and thickened. Mix the remaining ingredients in a large bowl. Add the chicken and mix well. Pour in the dressing and toss until all the ingredients are well coated with the dressing. Serve immediately. Enjoy!

Grilled Chicken and Arugula Salad

Ingredients

8, 6-ounce skinless, boneless chicken breast halves
1/2 tsp. salt
1/2 tsp. black pepper
Cooking spray
10 cups arugula
2 cup multicolored cherry tomatoes, halved
1/2 cup thinly sliced red onion
1/2 cup olive oil and vinegar salad dressing, divided
20 pitted kalamata olives, chopped
1 cup crumbled goat cheese

Method

Season the chicken breast with salt and pepper. Spray a grill pan with some cooking spray and heat it on medium high heat. Place the chicken on the pan and cook until done. Keep aside. In a bowl mix together the tomatoes, arugula, onion, olives and 6 tbsp. dressing. Brush the remaining dressing on the chicken and cut into slices. Mix the chicken and tomato arugula mix and toss well. Serve immediately.   Enjoy!

Seashell Pasta Salad with Buttermilk-Chive Dressing

Ingredients

2 cups uncooked seashell pasta
2 cups frozen green peas
1/2 cup organic canola mayonnaise
1/2 cup fat-free buttermilk
2 tbsp. minced fresh chives
2 tsp. chopped fresh thyme
1 tsp. salt
1 tsp. freshly ground black pepper
4 garlic cloves, minced
4 cups loosely packed baby arugula
2 tsp. olive oil
4 ounces finely chopped prosciutto, about 1/2 cup

Method

Prepare the pasta according to the manufacturer's instructions. When the pasta is almost cooked, add in the peas and cook for 2 minutes. Drain and dunk in cold water. Drain again. In a bowl combine the mayonnaise, buttermilk, chives, thyme, salt, pepper and garlic and mix well. Add in the pasta and peas and arugula to it and mix well. Sauté the prosciutto in a skillet over medium high heat until crisp. Sprinkle over salad and serve. Enjoy!

Arctic Char with Tomato Vinaigrette

Ingredients

8, 6-ounce arctic char fillets
1 1/2 tsp. salt, divided
1 tsp. black pepper, divided
Cooking spray
8 tsp. balsamic vinegar

4 tbsp. extra-virgin olive oil
4 tsp. minced shallots
2 pint grape tomatoes, halved
10 cups loosely packed arugula
4 tbsp. pine nuts, toasted

Method

Season the arctic char fillets with some salt and pepper. Cook them in a skillet for about 4 minutes on both sides. Remove the fillets from the pan and cover with a paper towel. Clean the pan off its juices. Pour the vinegar in a small bowl. Slowly drizzle in the oil and whisk until it thickens. Add in the shallots and mix well. Add the tomatoes, salt and pepper to the pan and heat it on a high flame and cook until the tomatoes soften. Add the dressing and mix well. While serving arrange a bed of arugula on the plate, place the arctic char and spoon out the tomato mix on each fillet. Top with some nuts and serve immediately. Enjoy!

Delicious Crab Salad

Ingredients

2 tbsp. grated lemon rind
10 tbsp. fresh lemon juice, divided
2 tbsp. extra virgin olive oil
2 tsp. honey
1 tsp. Dijon mustard
1/2 tsp. salt
1/4 tsp. freshly ground black pepper
2 cups fresh corn kernels, about 2 ears

1/2 cup thinly sliced basil leaves
1/2 cup chopped red bell pepper
4 tbsp. finely chopped red onion
2 pound lump crabmeat, shell pieces removed
16, 1/4-inch-thick slices ripe beefsteak tomato
4 cups cherry tomatoes, halved

Method

In a large bowl mix together the rind, 6 tbsp. lemon juice, olive oil, honey, mustard, salt and pepper. Remove about 3 tbsp. of this mixture and set aside. Add in the remaining 6tbsp. lemon juice, corn, basil, red bell pepper, red onion and crab meat to the remaining juice mix and mix well. Add in the tomatoes and cherry tomatoes and toss well. Just before serving pour the retained juice over it and serve immediately. Enjoy!

Chicken Orzo Salad

Ingredients

1cup uncooked orzo
1/2 tsp. grated lemon rind
6 tbsp. fresh lemon juice
2 tbsp. extra-virgin olive oil
1 tsp. kosher salt
1 tsp. minced garlic
1/2 tsp. honey
1/4 tsp. freshly ground black pepper

2 cups shredded skinless, boneless rotisserie chicken breast
1 cup diced English cucumber
1 cup red bell pepper
2/3 cup thinly sliced green onions
2 tbsp. chopped fresh dill
1 cup crumbled goat cheese

Method

Prepare the orzo according to the manufacturer's instructions. Drain and dunk in cold water and drain again and put in a large bowl. Combine the lemon rind, lemon juice, oil, kosher, garlic, honey and pepper in a bowl. Whisk together until combined. Pour this mix over the prepared pasta and mix well. Mix in the chicken, cucumber, red bell pepper, green onions and dill. Toss well. Top with cheese and serve immediately. Enjoy!

Halibut and Peach Salad

Ingredients

6 tbsp. extra-virgin olive oil, divided
8, 6-ounce halibut fillets
1 tsp. kosher salt, divided
1 tsp. freshly ground black pepper, divided
4 tbsp. chopped fresh mint
4 tbsp. fresh lemon juice

2 tsp. maple syrup
12 cups baby spinach leaves
4 medium peaches, halved and sliced
1 English cucumber, halved lengthwise and sliced
1/2 cup toasted sliced almonds

Method

Sprinkle the halibut fillets with some salt and pepper. Place the fish on a heated skillet and cook on both sides for 6 minutes or until the fish lightly flakes when cut with a fork. In a large bowl mix together the salt, pepper, oil, lemon juice, mint and maple syrup and whisk until combined. Add the baby spinach, peaches and cucumber to it and toss well. While serving, serve the fillet on a bed of the salad and top with some almonds.   Enjoy!

Beet and Blue Cheese Salad

Ingredients

2 cup torn fresh mint leaves
2/3 cup thinly vertically sliced red onion
2, 6-ounce package baby kale
1/2 cup plain 2% reduced-fat Greek yogurt
4 tbsp. fat-free buttermilk
4 tsp. white wine vinegar
3 tsp. extra-virgin olive oil
1/2 tsp. kosher salt
1/2 tsp. freshly ground black pepper
8 hard-cooked large eggs, quartered lengthwise
2, 8-ounce package peeled and steamed baby beets, quartered
1 cup coarsely chopped walnuts
4 ounces blue cheese, crumbled

Method

In a large bowl mix together the onion, kale, eggs, beet and mint. In another bowl mix together the Greek yoghurt, buttermilk, vinegar, oil, salt and pepper. Whisk until all the ingredients are well incorporated. Just before serving pour the dressing over the salad and serve garnished with the walnuts and cheese.

Italian Style Green Salad

Ingredients

4 cups romaine lettuce - torn, washed and dried
2 cups torn escarole
2 cups torn radicchio
2 cups torn red leaf lettuce
1/2 cup chopped green onions
1 red bell pepper, sliced into rings
1 green bell pepper, sliced in rings
24 cherry tomatoes
1/2 cup grapeseed oil
1/4 cup chopped fresh basil
1/2 cup balsamic vinegar
1/4 cup lemon juice
salt and pepper to taste

Method

For the salad: Mix together the romaine lettuce, escarole, red leaf lettuce, radicchio, scallions, cherry tomatoes, green bell pepper and red bell pepper in a bowl.
For the dressing: in a small bowl combine the basil, balsamic vinegar, grapeseed oil, lemon juice and mix well. Season with salt and pepper.
Just before serving pour the dressing on the salad and toss well to coat. Serve immediately. Enjoy!

Broccoli Salad with Cranberries

Ingredients

1/4 cup balsamic vinegar
2 tsp. Dijon mustard
2 tsp. maple syrup
2 cloves garlic, minced
1 tsp. grated lemon zest
salt and pepper to taste

1 cup canola oil
2, 16 ounce packages broccoli coleslaw mix
1 cup dried cranberries
1/2 cup chopped green onions
1/2 cup chopped pecans

Method

Pour the vinegar in a medium sized bowl. Add in the Dijon mustard, garlic, lemon zest and maple syrup to it. Whisk well and gradually stream in the oil and whisk until combined. Add the broccoli slaw, green onions, dried cranberries and onion in a large mixing bowl. Drizzle the dressing over the salad and toss well. Place in the fridge and chill for half an hour. Top with pecans and serve immediately. Enjoy!

Delicious Marconi Salad

Ingredients

2 cups uncooked elbow macaroni
1/2 cup mayonnaise
2 tbsp. distilled white vinegar
1/3 cup white sugar
1 tbsp. and 3/4 tsp. prepared yellow mustard
3/4 tsp. salt

1/4 tsp. ground black pepper
1/2 large onion, chopped
1 stalk celery, chopped
1/2 green bell pepper, seeded and chopped
2 tbsp. grated carrot, optional
1 tbsp. chopped pimento peppers, optional

Method

Prepare the macaroni according to the manufacturer's instructions. Drain, dunk in cold water and drain again. Combine the mayonnaise, sugar, mustard, vinegar, pepper and salt in a large bowl. Add in the green bell pepper, celery, pimentos, carrot and the macaroni and mix well. Chill overnight before serving. Enjoy!

Potato and Bacon Salad

Ingredients

1 pound clean, scrubbed new red potatoes   3 eggs

1/2 pound bacon
1/2 onion, finely chopped
1/2 stalk celery, finely chopped

1 cup mayonnaise
salt and pepper to taste

Method

Cook the potatoes in boiling water until tender. Drain and cool in the fridge. Hard boil the eggs in some boiling water, dunk in cold water, peel and chop. Brown the bacon in a skillet. Drain and crumble into smaller pieces. Chop up the cold potatoes into bite sized pieces. Combine all the ingredients in a large bowl. Serve chilled. Enjoy!

Roquefort Lettuce Salad

Ingredients

2 heads leaf lettuce, torn into bite-size pieces
6 pears - peeled, cored and chopped
10 ounces Roquefort cheese, crumbled
2 avocado - peeled, pitted, and diced
1 cup thinly sliced green onions
1/2 cup white sugar
1 cup pecans

2/3 cup olive oil
1/4 cup and 2 tbsp. red wine vinegar
1 tbsp. white sugar
1 tbsp. prepared mustard
2 cloves garlic, chopped
1 tsp. salt
Fresh ground black pepper to taste

Method

Add the 1/2cup sugar with the pecans in a skillet. Cook on a medium heat until the sugar melts and the pecans caramelize. Slowly pour the mix onto a waxed paper and cool. Break into pieces and keep aside. Pour the olive oil, red wine vinegar, 1 tbsp. sugar, mustard, garlic, pepper and salt in a food processor and process until all the ingredients are incorporated. In a large salad bowl add all the leftover ingredients and pour in the dressing. Toss well to coat. Top with the caramelized pecans and serve. Enjoy!

Tuna Salad

Ingredients

2, 7 ounce cans white tuna, drained and flaked
3/4 cup mayonnaise or salad dressing
2 tbsp. Parmesan cheese
1/4 cup and 2 tbsp. sweet pickle relish

1/4 tsp. dried minced onion flakes
1/2 tsp. curry powder
2 tbsp. dried parsley
2 tsp. dried dill weed
2 pinches garlic powder

Method

Add the white tuna, mayonnaise, Parmesan, sweet pickle relish and onion pickles in a medium sized bowl. Mix well. Sprinkle the curry powder, parsley, dill weed and garlic powder and toss well. Serve immediately. Enjoy!

Antipasto Pasta Salad

Ingredients

2 pounds seashell pasta
1/2 pound Genoa salami, chopped
1/2 pound pepperoni sausage, chopped
1 pound Asiago cheese, diced
2, 6 ounce cans black olives, drained and chopped
2 red bell pepper, diced
2 green bell pepper, chopped
6 tomatoes, chopped

2, .7 ounce packages dry Italian-style salad dressing mix
1-1/2 cups extra virgin olive oil
1/2 cup balsamic vinegar
1/4 cup dried oregano
2 tbsp. dried parsley
2 tbsp. grated Parmesan cheese
Salt and ground black pepper to taste

Method

Cook the pasta according to the manufacturer's instructions. Drain and dunk in cold water. Drain again. Add the pasta, pepperoni, salami, black olives, Asiago cheese, tomatoes, red bell pepper and green bell pepper in a large bowl. Mix well. Sprinkle the dressing mix and toss well. Cover with a cling wrap and chill.
For the dressing: Pour the olive oil, oregano, balsamic vinegar, Parmesan cheese, parsley, pepper and salt in a bowl. Whisk well until combined. Just before you serve, drizzle the dressing over the salad and toss to coat. Serve immediately. Enjoy!

Sesame Pasta Chicken Salad

Ingredients

1/2 cup sesame seeds
2, 16 ounce packages bow tie pasta
1 cup vegetable oil
2/3 cup light soy sauce
2/3 cup rice vinegar
2 tsp. sesame oil
1/4 cup and 2 tbsp. white sugar
1 tsp. ground ginger
1/2 tsp. ground black pepper

6 cups shredded, cooked chicken breast meat
2/3 cup chopped fresh cilantro
2/3 cup chopped green onion

Method

Lightly toast the sesame seeds in a skillet over medium high heat until the aroma fills the kitchen. Keep aside. Cook the pasta according to the manufacturer's instructions. Drain, dunk in cold water and drain and place in a bowl. Blend the vegetable oil, rice vinegar, soy sauce, sugar, sesame oil, ginger, pepper and sesame seeds together until all the ingredients are incorporated. Pour the prepared dressing over the pasta and mix well until the dressing coats the pasta. Add in the green onions, cilantro and chicken and mix well. Serve immediately. Enjoy!

Traditional Potato Salad

Ingredients

10 potatoes
6 eggs
2 cups chopped celery
1 cup chopped onion
1 cup sweet pickle relish

1/2 tsp. garlic salt
1/2 tsp. celery salt
2 tbsp. prepared mustard
Ground black pepper to taste
1/2 cup mayonnaise

Method

Cook the potatoes in a pot of boiling salinated water until tender, but not mushy. Drain the water and peel the potatoes. Chop into bite sized pieces. Hard boil the eggs and peel and chop them. Combine all the ingredients together in a large bowl gently. Do not be too rough or else you will end up smashing the potatoes and eggs. Serve chilled. Enjoy!

Quinoa Tabbouleh

Ingredients

4 cups water
2 cups quinoa
2 pinches salt
1/2 cup olive oil
1 tsp. sea salt
1/2 cup lemon juice

6 tomatoes, diced
2 cucumber, diced
4 bunches green onions, diced
4 carrots, grated
2 cups fresh parsley, chopped

Method

Boil some water in a saucepan. Add a pinch of salt and the quinoa to it. Cover the saucepan with a lid and let the liquid simmer for about 15-20 minutes. Once cooked, take off heat and mix around with a fork to cool it faster. While the quinoa cools, place the rest of the ingredients in a large bowl. Add in the cooled quinoa and mix well. Serve immediately. Enjoy!

Frozen Salad

Ingredients

2 cups yoghurt
2 cups fresh cream
1 cup cooked macaroni
2-3 chilies, chopped

3 tbsp. chopped cilantro
3 tsp. sugar
Salt to taste

Method

Combine all the ingredients in a large mixing bowl and refrigerate overnight. Serve chilled.   Enjoy!

Strawberry and Feta Salad

Ingredients

1/2 cup slivered almonds
1 clove garlic, minced
1/2 tsp. honey
1/2 tsp. Dijon mustard
2 tbsp. raspberry vinegar
1 tbsp. balsamic vinegar

1 tbsp. brown sugar
1/2 cup vegetable oil
1/2 head romaine lettuce, torn
1 cup fresh strawberries, sliced
1/2 cup crumbled feta cheese

Method

Roast the almonds in a skillet over a medium flame. Keep aside. Combine the honey, garlic, mustard, the two vinegars, vegetable oil and brown sugar in a bowl. Mix all the ingredients with the toasted almonds in a large salad bowl. Pour the dressing just before serving, toss well to coat and serve immediately. Enjoy!

Cooling Cucumber Salad

Ingredients

2 large cucumbers, cut into ½ inch pieces
1 cup full fat yoghurt
2 tsp. dill weed, chopped finely
Salt to taste

Method

Whisk the yoghurt until smooth. Add in the cucumber, dill weed and salt and mix well. Chill overnight and serve topped with some dill. Enjoy!

Colorful Salad

Ingredients

2 cups corn kernels, boiled
1 green bell pepper, diced
1 red bell pepper, diced
1 yellow bell pepper, diced
2 tomatoes, de-seeded, diced

2 potatoes, boiled, diced
1 cup lemon juice
2 tsp. dry mango powder
Salt to taste
2 tbsp. cilantro, chopped, to garnish

Method

Combine all the ingredients except for the cilantro in a large mixing bowl. Season to taste. Chill overnight. Top with cilantro just before serving. Enjoy!

Garbanzo Bean Salad

Ingredients

1, 15 ounce can garbanzo beans, drained
1 cucumbers, halved lengthwise and sliced
6 cherry tomatoes, halved
1/4 red onion, chopped
1 clove garlic, minced
1/2, 15 ounce can black olives, drained and chopped

1/2 ounce crumbled feta cheese
1/4 cup Italian-style salad dressing
1/4 lemon, juiced
1/4 tsp. garlic salt
1/4 tsp. ground black pepper
1 tbsp. cream for garnish

Method

Mix all the ingredients together in a large mixing bowl and place in the refrigerator for at least 3 hours before serving.
Combine the beans, cucumbers, tomatoes, red onion, garlic, olives, cheese, salad dressing, lemon juice, garlic salt and pepper. Toss together and refrigerate 2 hours before serving. Serve chilled. Serve topped with the cream. Enjoy!

Tangy Avocado and Cucumber Salad

Ingredients

4 medium cucumbers, cubed
4 avocados, cubed
1/2 cup chopped fresh cilantro
2 cloves garlic, minced
1/4 cup minced green onions, optional

1/2 tsp. salt
black pepper to taste
1/2 large lemon
2 limes

Method

Combine all the ingredients except for the lime juice in a large mixing bowl. Refrigerate for at least an hour. Pour the lime juice on the salad just before serving and serve immediately. Enjoy!

Basil, Feta and Tomato Salad

Ingredients

12 roma, plum tomatoes, diced
2 small cucumber - peeled, quartered lengthwise, and chopped
6 green onions, chopped
1/2 cup fresh basil leaves, cut into thin strips

1/4 cup and 2 tbsp. olive oil
1/4 cup balsamic vinegar
1/4 cup and 2 tbsp. crumbled feta cheese
salt and freshly ground black pepper to taste

Method

Combine all the ingredients together in a large salad bowl. Adjust seasoning according to taste and serve immediately. Enjoy!

Pasta and Spinach Salad

Ingredients

1/2, 12 ounce package farfalle pasta
5 ounces baby spinach, rinsed and torn into bite-size piece
1 ounce crumbled feta cheese with basil and tomato
1/2 red onion, chopped
1/2, 15 ounce can black olives, drained

and chopped
1/2 cup Italian-style salad dressing
2 cloves garlic, minced
1/2 lemon, juiced
1/4 tsp. garlic salt
1/4 tsp. ground black pepper

Method

Prepare pasta according to the manufacturer's instruction. Drain and dunk in cold water. Drain again and place in a large mixing bowl. Add in the spinach, cheese, olives and red onions. In another bowl combine the salad dressing, lemon juice, garlic, pepper and garlic salt together. Whisk until combined. Pour over the salad and serve immediately. Enjoy!

Basil and Sun Dried Tomato Orzo

Ingredients

1 cup uncooked orzo pasta
1/4 cup chopped fresh basil leaves
2 tbsp. and 2 tsp. chopped oil-packed sun-dried tomatoes
1 tbsp. olive oil

1/4 cup and 2 tbsp. grated Parmesan cheese
1/4 tsp. salt
1/4 tsp. ground black pepper

Method

Prepare pasta according to the manufacturer's instruction. Drain and dunk in cold water. Drain again and keep aside. In a food processor place the sun dried tomatoes and basil and blend until smooth. Combine all the ingredients in a large bowl and toss well. Season to taste. This salad can be served at room temperature or chilled. Enjoy!

Creamy Chicken Salad

Ingredients

2 cups mayonnaise
2 tbsp. sugar, or more depending on the sweetness of your mayonnaise
2 tsp. pepper
1 chicken breast, boneless and skinless

1 pinch garlic powder
1 pinch onion powder
1 tbsp. chopped cilantro
Salt, to taste

Method

Pan fry the chicken breast until cooked. Cool and chop into bite sized pieces. Combine all the ingredients in a large bowl and toss well. Season according to taste and serve chilled. Enjoy!

Refreshing Green Gram and Yoghurt Challenge

Ingredients

2 cups green gram
1 cup thick yoghurt
1 tsp. chili powder

2 tbsp. sugar
Salt, to taste

Method

Boil a pot of water and add a pinch of salt and the green gram to it. Cook until almost done and drain. Rinse under cold water and set aside. Whisk the yoghurt until smooth. Add the chili powder, sugar and salt to it and mix well. Chill the yoghurt in the fridge for a few hours. Just before serving scoop out the green gram in a serving plate and serve topped with the prepared yoghurt. Serve immediately. Enjoy!

Avocado and Arugula Salad Topped with Crumbled Feta

Ingredients

1 ripe avocado, washed
A handful of arugula leaves
1 pink grapefruit, seeds removed
½ cup feta cheese, crumbled

3 tbsp. balsamic vinegar
4 tbsp. olive oil
1 tsp. mustard

Method

Scoop out the fleshy part of the avocado and place in a bowl. Add the balsamic vinegar and olive oil to it and whisk until smooth. Add in rest of the ingredients except for the feta cheese and toss well. Serve topped with the crumbled feta cheese. Enjoy!

Sprouted Green Gram Salad

Ingredients

1 cup green gram sprouts
1/4 cup seeded, diced cucumber
1/4 cup seeded, chopped tomato
2 tbsp. and 2 tsp. chopped green onions
1 tbsp. chopped fresh cilantro
1/4 cup thinly sliced radishes, optional
1-1/2 tsp. olive oil
1 tbsp. lemon juice

1-1/2 tsp. white wine vinegar
3/4 tsp. dried oregano
1/4 tsp. garlic powder
3/4 tsp. curry powder
1/4 tsp. dry mustard
1/2 pinch salt and pepper to taste

Method

Combine all the ingredients in a large mixing bowl and toss until all the ingredients are coated with the oil. Chill in the refrigerator for a few hours before serving. Enjoy!

Healthy Chickpea Salad

Ingredients

2-1/4 pounds chickpeas, drained
1/4 cup red onion, chopped
4 cloves garlic, minced
2 tomato, chopped

1 cup chopped parsley
1/4 cup and 2 tbsp. olive oil
2 tbsp. lemon juice
salt and pepper to taste

Method

Combine all the ingredients in a large mixing bowl and toss well. Refrigerate overnight. Serve chilled. Enjoy!

Bacon and Pea Salad with a Ranch Dressing

Ingredients

8 slices bacon
8 cups water
2, 16 ounce packages frozen green peas

2/3 cup chopped onions
1 cup Ranch dressing
1 cup shredded Cheddar cheese

Method

Brown the bacon in a large skillet on high heat. Drain the fat and crumble the bacon and keep aside. In a large pot boil some water and add the peas to it. Cook the peas for just a minute and drain. Dunk in cold water and drain again. In a large bowl combine the crumbled bacon, boiled peas, onion, Cheddar cheese and Ranch dressing. Toss well and refrigerate. Serve chilled. Enjoy!

Crispy Asparagus Salad

Ingredients

1-1/2 tsp. rice vinegar
1/2 tsp. red wine vinegar
1/2 tsp. soy sauce
1/2 tsp. white sugar
1/2 tsp. Dijon mustard

1 tbsp. peanut oil
1-1/2 tsp. sesame oil
3/4 pound fresh asparagus, trimmed and cut into 2-inch pieces
1-1/2 tsp. sesame seeds

Method

In a small mixing bowl add the rice vinegar, rice wine vinegar, sugar, soy sauce and mustard. Slowly pour in the oils, while you continuously whisk it, in order to emulsify the liquids together. Fill a pot with water and add a pinch of salt to it. Bring to a boil. Put in the asparagus in the water and cook for 5 minutes or until tender but not mushy. Drain and dunk in cold water. Drain again and place in a large bowl. Pour the prepared dressing over the asparagus and mix until the dressing coats the asparagus. Top with some sesame seeds and serve immediately. Enjoy!

Conclusion

The book has been written for those people who are not only health conscious, but also for those people who want to prepare exciting dishes for day to day consumption. Veggies are not only full of roughage and fibers, but also help in maintaining a balanced diet. The ingredients used in the recipes in this book are given in precise quantities, making it easy for you to cook your dish. The best thing about the book is that with the ingredients are also the most cheaply available products in the market. Each and every ingredient can be gathered from the market, and I have also written my different experiments with texture and taste. In the book you will also find that salads are not just limited to pieces of lettuce. The dishes gives you a fine dining experience, while making sure you eat healthy and receive the perfect nutrition.

Thank you again for purchasing this book!

Finally, if you enjoyed this book, please take the time to share your thoughts and post a review on Amazon. It'd be greatly appreciated!

Feel free to contact me at emma.katie@outlook.com

Check out more books by Emma Katie at:

www.amazon.com/author/emmakatie